Castle of Roccascalenga, Abruzzo

Food lover Silvia Colloca is a woman of many talents: professional actress, trained opera singer, published author, blogger and sensational cook. After spending her childhood in the kitchens of her mother and grandmothers, Silvia absorbed much of their Italian culinary heritage. Since moving to Australia several years ago, Silvia has kneaded, beaten, rolled, chopped and pounded her way to an authentic Italian identity in her Sydney kitchen. Silvia is married to actor Richard Roxburgh and they have two sons, Raphael and Miro. Silvia's successful first cookbook, *Silvia's Cucina*, was published in 2013, and she has just finished filming her debut television series, *Made in Italy with Silvia Colloca*, which will air on SBS.

silviascucina.net

My handsome Papà and me, sipping coffee at Penna Nera bar in Torricella Peligna.

MADE IN ITALY

with Silvia Colloca

Location photography by Carla Coulson

Recipe photography by Chris Chen

LANTERN

an imprint of
PENGUIN BOOKS

This book is dedicated to all who share
my all-consuming love for genuine
food and the legacy that comes with it.
Love, Silvia

Cousin Miriam giving me a pasta-making masterclass.

Lake Barnea, Abruzzo

Caciocavallo cheese, Agnone, Molise

The streets of
Macerata, Marche

Barrea, Abruzzo

• CONTENTS •

MY JOURNEY BACK TO CENTRAL ITALY 1

MARCHE

Focaccia con cipolle 18
Focaccia with stewed onion

Ciabatta di farro 20
Spelt ciabatta

Olive all'ascolana 22
Stuffed fried olives

**SOURCING THE BEST VEGETABLES
AT THE LOCAL MERCATO ORTOFRUTTICOLO** 24

Zucchine gratinate 27
Zucchini gratin

Gnocchi con zucchine e pecorino 28
Potato gnocchi with zucchini and pecorino

Piselli, prosciutto e lattuga 30
Stewed peas with prosciutto and baby lettuce

Minestrone primavera 33
Spring vegetable minestrone

A TRIP TO SAN BENEDETTO DEL TRONTO ... 36

Fritto misto 39
Crispy fried prawns and calamari

Gamberi gratinati 40
Gratinated prawns with lemon and parsley

Strozzapreti con rana pescatrice 42
Handmade noodles with monkfish ragù

Calamari in guazzetto 45
Calamari with tomatoes and wine

Polipo con patate 46
Octopus and potato salad

Patate arrosto con alloro e guanciale ... 52
Roast potatoes with bay leaves and cured pork cheek

Coniglio in porchetta 54
Rolled deboned rabbit

Pollo in potacchio 56
Braised chicken marylands with wine and tomatoes

Pollo alla boscaiola 59
Woodsman's chicken

Coratella di agnello 60
Sautéed lamb offal

Vincisgrassi 62
Lasagne Marche style

Torta all'olio e albicocche 66
Apricot and olive oil cake

Ciambellone di limone e ricotta 69
Lemon and ricotta ring cake

Tozzetti 70
Almond and lemon biscotti

ABRUZZO

Pizza scima 86
White wine unleavened bread

Pizzelle salate con vino 90
Savoury white wine and olive oil waffles

Pallotte cacio e ovo 92
Stale bread and pecorino dumplings

MAMMA AND PAPÀ'S ARTICHOKE RECIPES 96

Insalata di carciofi e pecorino 99
Raw artichoke and shaved pecorino salad

Tortino di carciofi gratinato 100
Artichoke gratin

Carciofi in padella 102
Sautéed artichokes

Frittata alle erbe con caprino 107
Herb frittata with goat's curd

Pizza rustica con bietola 108
Savoury tart with chard

Fagioli e rape 110
Broccoli rabe and borlotti beans

Peperonata 112
Sweet and sour capsicum

Calzoni con caciocavallo e peperonata 114
Bread pockets with cheese and stewed capsicum

Maccheroni alla chitarra con fiori di zucca e zafferano 117
Noodles with zucchini blossom and saffron sauce

COUSIN MIRIAM'S RECIPES 122

Tacconcelli con ragù di pesce 126
Homemade pasta squares with fish stew

Cozze ripiene con chitarrina 128
Homemade spaghetti with stuffed mussels

Pizza con frutti di mare 132
Seafood pizza

'mpepata di cozze 138
Mussels in pepper broth

Ditalini risottati con vongole e ceci 140
Ditalini with clams and chickpeas, cooked risotto-style

Pasta rotta con lenticchie 143
Broken pasta and lentil soup

Scrippelle 'mbusse 144
Crepes in broth

Sagne e fasciul' 148
Pasta and bean soup

Le virtù 150
Cereal soup

AGRITURISMO TROILO 152

Cannelloni di Antonina 157
Antonina's cannelloni with braised meat

Arrosticini 159
Mini sheep skewers

Agnello cacio e ovo 163
Lamb with egg, lemon and cheese sauce

Agnello alla griglia con asparagi 164
Grilled lamb chops with asparagus

Celli pieni 166
Grape jam crescents

Calcionetti 170
Chickpea and honey pastries

Tartellette allo zafferano 174
Saffron tartlets

Bocconotti 176
Filled short pastries

Pan dell'orso 178
Bear's cake

Fiadone di Vincenzo 181
Vincenzo's fiadone cake

Pizza dolce 182
Celebration sponge cake

Cicerchiata 184
Honey-drizzled cluster cake

Pesche al vino con crema di mascarpone 188
Wine-drenched peaches with mascarpone cream

MOLISE

Pizza di San Martino 205
Saint Martin rolls

Panini all'olio 206
Olive oil bread crescents

Crostini con ricotta e spinaci 210
Crostini with lemon ricotta and spinach

Pizza di farro con soppressata e patate 212
No-knead spelt pizza with soppressata and potatoes

HOMEMADE CHEESE 216

Primo sale 218
Homemade primo sale cheese

Primo sale alla piastra con verdure 220
Grilled primo sale and vegetable salad

Ricotta fatta in casa 223
Homemade ricotta

Crostata con ricotta, cioccolato e ciliege 224
Ricotta, chocolate and cherry tart

I rose ch'à pastella 229
Battered cauliflower florets

Peperoni imbottiti 230
Stuffed capsicum

Broccolini ripassati 232
Broccolini cooked with chilli and garlic

Insalata di lenticchie e peperoni 237
Lentil and capsicum salad

Ceci in umido 238
Chickpea stew

Zuppa di cipolle 243
Onion stew

Tagliolini ai ricci di mare 244
Homemade tagliolini with sea urchin roe

I polpe 'npergatori 246
Octopus in purgatory (aka Spicy baby octopus stew)

Crostacei all' agro 248
Crustacea with lemon, garlic and parsley sauce

Ragù di capra con malefante 252
Fresh pasta strips with slow-cooked goat sauce

Cavatelli lunghi alla molisana 254
Handmade pasta with slow-cooked meat sauce

Agnello in brodo con piselli e fave 258
Lamb in broth with peas and broad beans

La pezzata 261
Sheep stew

Mostaccioli 264
Honey, chocolate and nutmeg cookies

Pesche di Castelbottaccio 266
Sponge cakes from Castelbottaccio

Torta di noci e cioccolato 268
Flourless walnut cake

Torta di mele della Signora Pia 270
Signora Pia's apple cake

ACKNOWLEDGEMENTS 276

INDEX 279

◆ ◆ ◆

MY JOURNEY BACK TO CENTRAL ITALY

◆ ◆ ◆ ◆ ◆ ◆ ◆

I spent the first 28 years of my life in Italy, a thoroughbred Italian girl, raised in Milan by a northern Italian Papà and an Abruzzese Mamma. But it was only since moving to Australia in the mid-noughties that I began to truly appreciate my cultural heritage.

As a young woman, I had became so frustrated with all the paradoxes and strife that make Italy such a difficult country to live in (Berlusconi, to name but one!) that I couldn't see or appreciate the great beauty of my homeland. It was only when I became a citizen of another country that I reconciled with my own. Suddenly I found myself missing everything about Italy: my family, the melodic sound of the language, the mad excitement around the annual Sanremo music festival, the landscape and, most importantly, the food. It seems I had to flee Italy to learn to love it.

My craving for Italy and my heritage has became stronger still since the birth of my two boys. Although I am thrilled to raise them in such a great country as Australia, I also feel the need to imbue them with a sense of their Italian identity.

This is one of the main reasons I started my blog, Silvia's Cucina, in 2011. I wanted it to be a perpetual archive of family recipes and stories that would otherwise be lost. I was not prepared for the extraordinary support I would receive from the blogging community around the world, and the apparent need for readers to connect with authentic Italian cooking. The blog gave life to my first book of the same name, a collection of family recipes and stories intertwined with my new Australian life. I'm not a chef nor even a trained cook. I am simply Italian, and wish to offer an insight into authentic home cooking, which I hope will lead to a better understanding of what it is to be Italian. *Silvia's Cucina*, the book and the blog, allowed me to do that, but I soon found myself wanting to share more, to dig deeper into my Italian culinary inheritance.

The solution was pretty simple: I had to go back to the source!

The moment I got off the plane in Rome, I was on my way. My ears eagerly embraced the sound of the Italian language ringing in the air. The dark-eyed customs officer dazzled me with a friendly 'Buongiorno', and I welcomed the thought that my English was no longer needed. My brain excitedly switched back to Italian. I even noted that my posture changed: I held my head a little higher and a subtle but noticeable strut replaced my usual gawky walk. The discomfort of spending 24 hours in a crammed plane evaporated, and was quickly replaced with a sense of utter exhilaration. I was back home. And on a mission.

My sense of bliss was such that even the grumpy, humourless car-rental employee couldn't shake it. I drove out of the parking lot, flashed a cheerful goodbye smile (met with a grim nod of the head) and set off on my adventure. It was a crisp spring morning and the sun cast a pink light, rendering the usually gloomy Italian autostrada a vivid shade of pretty.

My mission was clear: travel, discover, taste, love and share. But because Italy is so rich and diverse, I had to limit this trip to a few regions. The urge to reconnect with my ancestral roots meant the choice was easy to make.

This was my journey back to central Italy.

The time I spent mingling with locals, perusing little markets and farms, or absorbing the sweeping landscapes was utterly inspiring. My visit to the lush Marche region was accented by the extraordinary conviviality of the people I met, so eager to share their memories, their recipes, their culinary dowry. It didn't seem strange to them that a woman from Australia sporting a thick Milanese accent would be so enthralled by their stories. Doors to their kitchens were thrown open in welcome and the wine flowed liberally to baptise new friendships. The hospitality of the Marchigiani is joyous, passionate and abundant. The local cuisine is a true reflection of the riches of a lucky territory, combined with a simple, deeply embedded understanding of what is good for you and what should (and should not) land on your plate. The Marchigiani like to call themselves 'buon gustai' (gourmands), and rightfully so!

Travelling south from Marche, the landscape gradually changed. The sweet, gentle valleys gave way to bolder shades of green and brown. The backdrop was dominated by snow-capped mountain peaks with the mighty Gran Sasso standing proudly amongst them. I was back in Abruzzo. I was home. Although I have returned to Mamma's village every year since I was a little girl, I was surprised at the trepidation I felt travelling there in pursuit of my food legacy.

Abruzzo is a gem amongst gems, a bountiful region of historical and artistic value, and brimming with superb produce. Abruzzo's true pride and glory lies in the simple fact that this is the Italy romantics dream of. Far from being postcard perfect, Abruzzo's appeal is linked to its dramatic landscapes, splendid cuisine and its inhabitants' famously unpretentious manner. Although the Abruzzesi may at first be guarded towards strangers, once they lose their initial reserve and trust is gained, they will open their hearts and homes with unparalleled generosity.

When I was a little girl I loved nothing more than returning to Mamma's village, Torricella Peligna, to visit my relatives. Although one should not have favourites, I couldn't help feeling a particular sense of kinship with my Great Aunt Italina, a formidable woman with a feisty personality. She hardly

old door in Barrea, Abruzzo

Mount Gran Sasso, Abruzzo

with Roberta and Quirino at
Hotel Paradiso, Torricella Peligna

Signor Fabrizio, the chivalrous
carabiniere, Pietrabbondante

my Raffi

patting Pasquale, Campobasso

4

spoke any Italian at all, and loved to launch into a long and involved rant at high speed in an indecipherable Abruzzese dialect. I barely understood a word, but I always found her enormously entertaining and endearing. She'd be looking out for me from her window and would cry, 'Ciacc' me! Quant si bell'! 'ma me, ti si fatt' gross'!', which more or less translates as 'My darling! You pretty thing! Look at you all grown up!' Without fail, she would invite me in and give me a few centrini (doilies) she'd been crocheting to add to my dowry, along with almond cookies and other lovelies.

Italina personified the very best of my Italy, which I know may soon become an antique Italy, one that might only be found in family stories or picture books. To me, it is a wild, generous and open-hearted Italy. But the other way this Italy is represented is, of course, in its food. So if I can unearth some beautiful local recipes and pass them on, perhaps in some very small way I can propagate the Italy I love.

My journey continued south of Abruzzo. I left behind the emerald-green mountain lakes, the fields of corn, almonds and garlic, for an untamed landscape populated by goats, dogs and lynxes. The countryside of Molise seems lost in time: unadorned, savage and striking, overlooked by Mount Meta, the largest of the massifs of south central Italy, with verdant hills covered in beech, maple and cherry trees. I immersed myself in the fascinating history of this region, once inhabited by tribes of ferocious warriors, and then invaded by the Romans. This legacy is ever-present in the ancient ruins that pepper its two provinces.

I wasn't really prepared for the warm welcome I was given in Molise. Once it became known that my intentions were genuine, people seemed to have an urge to tell me about their families, their stories, their love for this region. I will never forget my time in Campobasso, making friends with the elderly locals, keen to share the beauty of the old town with me. Even the dog, Pasquale, seemed keen to lend a paw! But perhaps my favourite moment happened when we got lost in Civitanova del Sannio. We parked the car in a tow zone to consult our map and were soon approached by a carabiniere (an Italian policeman). Instead of issuing a ticket, Mr Fabrizio escorted us back to Pietrabbondante and gave us his phone number in case we got lost again. Talk about good public service!

My journey back to central Italy has been one of self-discovery too. I observed, listened, smelt, felt and learnt. And the simplest, most efficient way to share this privilege is by inviting you to taste the flavours of Marche, Abruzzo and Molise, the strong, spirited and authentic core of Italy.

Con amore,

Silvia

Torricella Peligna, Abruzzo
(Mamma's village)

Recanati, Marche

MARCHE

— ◆ — MOTHER NATURE'S MASTERPIECE — ◆ —

Marche (pronounced Mar-kay), a verdant region safely enclosed by Emilia Romagna, Umbria and Abruzzo, seems to have received rather special treatment from Mother Nature. The lush, sweeping landscape is dispersed with medieval villages and gentle hills rolling down to the Adriatic plain. The soil is rich and bursting with spectacular local products. It is no surprise that the local cuisine is an absolute triumph of flavours. ✍

Culinary highlights include the robust rabbit in porchetta (see page 54), succulent and delicate octopus salad (see page 46) and of course one of the region's signature dishes, Vincisgrassi (see page 62), an indulgent layered pasta bake that dates back to 1799. The Marchigiani are very proud of their culinary identity. Their merry and opinionated personality is clearly reflected in the dishes they love to make, where the focus always comes back to one thing: the produce. And what an abundance of produce there is!

The waters of the Adriatic boast a splendid array of local seafood, such as bream, red mullet, snapper, squid, crayfish, crab and telline, the smallest, sweetest clams you may ever find. The inventive Marchigiani chefs and home cooks have devised the most flavoursome ways to enjoy them, including golden, crispy fritto misto (see page 39) and a show-stopping monkfish ragù (see page 42) – always a crowd pleaser.

Travelling inland, in the countryside around the old cities of Macerata and Ascoli Piceno truffles may be found growing in the shade of olive trees, which in turn are bursting with ripe fruit ready to be pressed into luscious extra virgin olive oil or stuffed and fried in one of the most delectable morsels I have ever tasted: the mighty olive all'ascolana (see page 22).

And I haven't even started on the wines, another marvel of Marche. Wine making here dates back thousands of years, to a time when the Etruscans farmed the land, grew prosperous vineyards and established fecund soil for us to enjoy all these years later. A little help from ideal weather conditions makes Marche an optimal place to grow grapes that will most likely be transformed into crisp white wine, such as Verdicchio or Pinot Grigio.

Yes, it is better I warn you now: if you are planning a culinary trip to these parts, pack your trainers and tracksuit pants and make sure you burn off some calories before or after gorging yourself on the regional delicacies! This is what I did when I went over to research the food and photograph the surroundings. I was not going to compromise on the authenticity of the recipes for the sake of my waistline. I had to taste them all, repeatedly. Then I had to cook them all, in various ways, adding ingredients, altering quantities (all the while remaining respectful of tradition) . . . Oh the dangers of recipe testing! Invariably I would finish an intense day of gluttony by running for miles, surrounded by the beautiful hills and the friendly but curious smiles of the locals, pointing at me saying, 'Corri, corri vardascia!' (Run, lady, run!). ✿

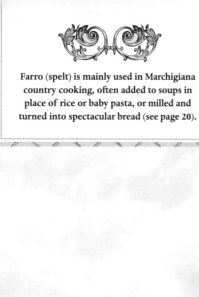

Farro (spelt) is mainly used in Marchigiana country cooking, often added to soups in place of rice or baby pasta, or milled and turned into spectacular bread (see page 20).

Montecassiano, Marche

Montecassiano, Marche

Marche sits where the ancient Picenum region once was. It became a Roman colony in 286 BC and famously sided with Rome against Hannibal during the epic Punic wars.

Italian fashionisti know where to find a bargain and Marche boasts the outlets of designer brands such as Tod's and Prada. My Uncle Claudio, a thoroughbred Milanese buisnessman with an eye for a sweet deal, never failed to take his late wife Rita for a shopping spree around there on their way back to Milan from their holidays in Abruzzo!

FOCACCIA con CIPOLLE

• FOCACCIA WITH STEWED ONION •

Italians can't let a day go by without bread. In fact I'll take this further and say that we really can't function without our daily intake of starch. This devotion has encouraged us to develop endless bread formulas and just when we thought we had nailed it with our ciabatta or pane di casa, some inventive baker came up with focaccia – a soft, bouncy creation that stands gloriously on its own, or can be embellished with sweet or savoury toppings. Stewed onion, flavoured with a hint of vin cotto and thyme makes a heavenly marriage.

SERVES 6

3 tablespoons extra virgin olive oil
3 red or brown onions, thinly sliced
3–4 sprigs thyme
pinch of salt flakes
1 scant tablespoon sugar
2 tablespoons vin cotto or balsamic vinegar

DOUGH
1 × 7 g sachet dried yeast
380 ml lukewarm water
2 teaspoons honey
3⅓ cups (500 g) plain, type '00' or baker's flour
2 tablespoons extra virgin olive oil
3 teaspoons salt flakes

1 To make the dough, dissolve the yeast in the water and stand for 5 minutes. Add the honey and mix well.

2 Put the flour in a large mixing bowl, pour in the yeast liquid and start mixing with a wooden spoon. Add the olive oil and salt, then tip the dough onto a floured cooking bench and knead for 8–10 minutes or until the dough is smooth and shiny. If you have a stand mixer fitted with a dough hook, you can let your appliance do the work for you in half the time.

3 Whichever method you use, the dough should feel slightly sticky. If it seems way too wet, add 1 tablespoon flour. Likewise, if it's too dry, add a little olive oil or water. All flours tend to vary slightly, even within the same brand, and you have to let your instincts guide you.

4 Shape the dough into a ball, then cover it with a moist tea towel and rest for 20 minutes. After this time, you will notice the dough has become shiny and elastic. Stretch it with your hands to form a rectangle, then fold it into three and shape it into a ball. Place the ball in an oiled bowl, cover with a moist tea towel and leave to prove for 1½–2 hours or until the dough has doubled in size.

5 Take the dough out of the bowl, flatten it gently with your hands and fold into three again. Rest the dough in a well-oiled baking dish (about 20 cm × 30 cm) for 1 hour or until airy, puffy and risen by one third. Using your fingers, gently push the dough to cover the baking dish, then dimple the surface with your fingertips.

• *This focaccia dough works just as well topped with cherry tomatoes and herbs.*

6 Meanwhile, prepare the stewed onion. Heat the olive oil in a large heavy-based saucepan over medium–high heat. Add the onion, thyme and a pinch of salt, then reduce the heat to low–medium and cook for 8–10 minutes, stirring gently, until the onion is soft and translucent. Add the sugar and vin cotto or vinegar and cook for another 2–3 minutes, then cover with a lid and cook over low heat for 10 minutes. Set aside.

7 Preheat your oven to 200°C (180°C fan-forced).

8 Spoon the stewed onion over the focaccia dough and bake for 20–25 minutes or until golden and puffy.

CIABATTA di FARRO

• SPELT CIABATTA •

Those of you familiar with my recipes won't be surprised to find me back with my hands in the dough, but for the new guests in my cucina, allow me to properly introduce myself: my name is Silvia Colloca and I am a bread-baking addict! Seriously, I often have three or four doughs at various stages of fermentation around the house, bubbling proudly in bowls on my shelves, above the fridge, sometimes spending the night in the warm comfort of my bedroom, to encourage excellent rising . . .

Recently I have developed a real passion for spelt flour, an ancient grain largely used in central Italy, which offers more nutritional value than plain white flour as well as a robust nutty flavour and a golden brown hue. Combine such qualities with the irresistible holey crumb and crackly crust of ciabatta and you'll understand why I'm often found in the kitchen at dawn, making sure my family and I can enjoy a few slices of this precious loaf for breakfast.

MAKES 1

1⅓ cups (200 g) spelt flour,
plus extra for dusting
2⅓ cups (350 g) strong
baker's flour
1 teaspoon dried yeast
425 ml water
2 teaspoons salt flakes
1 tablespoon olive oil

1 Place the flours in a large mixing bowl, add the yeast and mix it through. Slowly pour in the water and work with a wooden spoon to incorporate it into the flour. Add the salt and olive oil and keep mixing with a spatula for 5–10 minutes or until the dough is smooth and elastic. This is a rather sticky dough that can't be kneaded as such. If you have a stand mixer, use it! Fit it with the paddle attachment and mix the dough on medium speed for 3–4 minutes.

2 Oil the top of the dough to prevent a skin forming and cover with plastic film. Allow to rise at room temperature for 6–8 hours or overnight in the fridge until doubled in size. Let it come to room temperature before moving on to the next step.

3 Line a baking tray with baking paper. Using a spatula or dough scraper, tip the risen dough onto the baking tray and stretch it out to a rectangle about 30 cm × 8 cm. The dough will feel gluey and wet, but don't be tempted to mix in more flour. Simply dust some flour over the top, then cover with a cloth and leave to rest for 1 hour.

4 Preheat your oven to 220°C (200°C fan-forced) and place a metal bowl or skillet on the bottom shelf of the oven to heat up.

5 When the dough has rested place the tray in the oven, fill the metal bowl or skillet with cold water to create steam and immediately close the oven door. Bake for 30–35 minutes or

- *The typical large holes in the crumb of ciabatta bread become smaller when using spelt or wholemeal flour. If you are after bigger holes, use 100% baker's or plain flour.*

until well risen and crusty. Tap the bottom with your fingers – if it sounds hollow, the bread is cooked through; if not, bake it for a few more minutes. You can flip it upside down to encourage the bottom to crunch up. After all, who enjoys a soggy bottom?

6 Transfer the bread to a wire rack and leave to rest at room temperature for at least 1 hour before slicing into it (this will allow the crumb to dry slightly). Enjoy with piquant extra virgin olive oil, cold cuts of meat and cheese, or good old butter and your favourite jam.

OLIVE ALL'ASCOLANA

◆ STUFFED FRIED OLIVES ◆

This appetiser is one of the most representative of Marchigiana culinary traditions, and is superb accompanied by a chilled glass of white wine. Small and scrumptious, the perfect olive all'ascolana requires a fair bit of work and devotion, but if you want to impress your Italian friends (or indeed, your non-Italian friends!), you can't go past these golden, crunchy flavour bombs.

◇◇◇◇◇◇◇◇◇◇◇◇◇◇◇◇◇◇◇◇◇ MAKES 30 ◇◇◇◇◇◇◇◇◇◇◇◇◇◇◇◇◇◇◇◇◇

30 large green olives, pitted
4 eggs, plus extra if needed
2 cups (300 g) plain flour
⅔ cup (70 g) dried
　　breadcrumbs
sunflower oil, for deep-frying
salt flakes and lemon cheeks,
　　to serve

STUFFING
2 tablespoons extra virgin
　　olive oil
1 small brown onion,
　　roughly chopped
1 small carrot, roughly
　　chopped
1 small celery stick,
　　roughly chopped
150 g pork sausage meat,
　　removed from its casing
100 g chicken thigh fillet,
　　cut into cubes
150 ml white wine
salt flakes
2 tablespoons fresh
　　breadcrumbs (see page 27)
2 tablespoons freshly grated
　　parmigiano or pecorino
1 tablespoon finely chopped
　　flat-leaf parsley
¼ teaspoon freshly
　　grated nutmeg
finely grated zest of ½ lemon

1　Place the olives in a bowl of cold water for 30 minutes to get rid of the briny flavour. Dry them and set them aside.

2　To make the stuffing, heat the olive oil in a large frying pan over medium heat, add the onion, carrot and celery and cook until softened. Add the pork and chicken meat and brown well. Pour in the wine and cook over high heat for 1–2 minutes or until the alcohol has evaporated, then reduce the heat to low, season with salt and cook for 15–20 minutes or until the meat is cooked through. Remove from the heat and stir in the breadcrumbs, then set aside to cool for 10 minutes. Transfer the mixture to a food processor and blitz for 10–15 seconds to form a thick paste. Scrape the paste into a bowl and add the remaining ingredients. Taste for salt and adjust accordingly.

3　Beat the eggs, then mix 3 tablespoons of the beaten egg through the stuffing (reserve the rest for later). Rest for 30 minutes.

4　Cut a slit in each olive and fill with ½ teaspoon stuffing. Roll the filled olives in the flour, then in the reserved beaten egg, and finally in the breadcrumbs. Roll them one last time in egg and breadcrumbs to create a super-crunchy double coating. You may need to replace the breadcrumbs halfway through rolling, as the wet egg mixture will inevitably make it a bit too sticky to be workable. Likewise, you may need to add an extra egg or two if the olives absorb more than you predict.

5　Half-fill a large frying pan or deep-fryer with sunflower oil and heat over medium–high heat to 180°C or until a cube of bread browns in 15 seconds. Add the stuffed olives in batches and fry for 3–4 minutes or until golden. Remove with a slotted spoon and drain on paper towel. Sprinkle with salt flakes and serve hot or warm with lemon.

◇◇

◆　*You can double the quantities and freeze half the stuffed and crumbed olives for up to 4 weeks. Deep-fry from frozen when you need them.*

SOURCING THE BEST VEGETABLES AT THE LOCAL MERCATO ORTOFRUTTICOLO

◆ ◆ ◆ ◆ ◆ ◆ ◆

It is a known fact that Italy is blessed with phenomenal local produce. It is the combination of perfect soil, optimal climate and a healthy dose of pride that turns fruit and vegetables into edible jewels. Market stalls are filled with picture-perfect sustainable produce. The embedded Italian sense of aesthetic is ever present and you can't fail to be tantalised by these arrangements, often so striking they could pass as modern art installations.

One additional, fundamental marvel of Italian farmers' markets is that everything is so cheap. I am talking about 3 euros for a case of freshly picked artichokes, or a single euro for a huge bunch of broccoli rabe. It is a wonderland! So my advice is this: when in Italy, ditch the chain supermarkets and get to the nearest market for the ripest, freshest, most beautiful fruits of the earth you could ever dream of.

ZUCCHINE GRATINATE

◆ ZUCCHINI GRATIN ◆

When choosing zucchini, look for small, shiny and dark green ones that are firm to the touch. If you feel so inclined, they are ridiculously easy to grow. I know this because I am a terrible veggie patch gardener yet still manage to produce a healthy crop of these green beauties every year.

MAKES 8

3 cups (210 g) fresh breadcrumbs (preferably homemade – see Note)
2 cups (160 g) grated pecorino or parmigiano
1 clove garlic, finely chopped or minced
4–5 marjoram leaves
4–5 oregano leaves
1–2 tablespoons finely chopped flat-leaf parsley
3 tablespoons extra virgin olive oil, plus extra for drizzling
salt flakes and freshly ground black pepper
4 zucchini (courgettes)

1 Preheat your oven to 200°C (180°C fan-forced). Line a baking tray with baking paper.

2 Mix together the breadcrumbs, cheese, garlic, herbs and olive oil in a large mixing bowl. Season to taste with salt and pepper and set aside.

3 Cut the zucchini in half lengthways. Using a spoon or a paring knife, scoop out some of the flesh, then fill the zucchini shells with the breadcrumb mixture. Place on the prepared tray, drizzle with a little extra olive oil and bake for 30–35 minutes or until golden brown.

◆ *To make breadcrumbs, simply blitz stale bread in a food processor until coarsely chopped. The breadcrumbs will keep in the fridge for up to 1 week.*

GNOCCHI con ZUCCHINE e PECORINO

• POTATO GNOCCHI WITH ZUCCHINI AND PECORINO •

Small, young zucchini are perfect for this dish. If you can, try to find those still attached to their golden blossoms – they will make a welcome addition to the sauce. The stars of the dish, though, are the gnocchi. Before you panic at the thought of making them from scratch, let me assure you that they are dead easy to make as long as you use the right type of potatoes. Starchy ones like desiree or russet will ensure your gnocchi will be light and pillowy. Trust me – you will never use store-bought ones again!

⸰⸰⸰⸰⸰⸰⸰ SERVES 4 ⸰⸰⸰⸰⸰⸰⸰

3 tablespoons extra virgin olive oil
2 golden shallots, thinly sliced
pinch of salt flakes
3 zucchini (courgettes), sliced into thin rounds
1 clove garlic, skin on, bashed with the back of a knife
150 ml vegetable stock
1 cup (80 g) shaved pecorino
finely grated zest of 1 lemon

POTATO GNOCCHI
850 g starchy potatoes (such as desiree or russet), well washed
1 egg yolk
small pinch of salt flakes
¾–1 cup (110–150 g) plain flour, plus extra for dusting

• *Cooking garlic in its skin is very typical of Italian home cooking. The flavour will be imparted into the sauce without lingering on your breath.*

1 To make the gnocchi, put the potatoes (in their skins) in a large saucepan of cold salted water. Bring to the boil over high heat and cook for 35–40 minutes or until cooked through. Drain well, then peel the potatoes, using a paring knife if necessary as they will be very hot. Pass the potatoes through a ricer (or use a potato masher), then cool for 5–10 minutes. Add the egg yolk and salt, then start adding the flour, a little at a time. Depending on your potatoes and the type of flour you use, you may need to use a little more or less than indicated. You want a soft dough that is pliable and not sticky. I normally end up adding ¾ cup (110 g) and use the rest for dusting while I'm shaping the gnocchi. Don't be tempted to add too much flour otherwise your gnocchi will be heavy.

2 Cut the dough into 4–5 pieces, then roll them out on a surface dusted with flour and shape them into 2–3 cm thick logs. Cut each log into 2–3 cm pieces. You can leave them like that or roll them onto the tines of a floured fork, gently but like you mean it. (Alternatively, you can buy a wooden gnocchi roller from a kitchenware shop.) When you serve up, the ridges in the tine pattern will trap the sauce for the joy of your palate. Once you have rolled all your gnocchi, dust them with flour and set aside.

3 Bring a large saucepan of salted water to the boil while you make the sauce.

4 Heat the olive oil in a large heavy-based frying pan or wok over low–medium heat and gently fry the shallot and salt for 1–2 minutes. Add the zucchini and garlic and cook for 5–8 minutes, then pour in the stock and bring to a simmer.

Cook for 5 minutes or so to allow the flavours to mingle and the liquid to reduce slightly. Taste for salt and adjust accordingly, keeping in mind that the pecorino added at the end will give a salty kick. Remove from the heat and set aside.

5 Add the gnocchi to the boiling water in batches so you don't overcrowd the pan. As soon as they are cooked, they will float to the surface. Lift them out with a slotted spoon and drop them straight into the sauce, along with 1–2 tablespoons of the cooking water. Turn on the heat under the sauce and cook the gnocchi in the sauce for 1 minute, then remove from the heat and crown with pecorino shavings and lemon zest. Serve piping hot, preferably with a chilled glass of white wine.

PISELLI, PROSCIUTTO *e* LATTUGA

• STEWED PEAS WITH PROSCIUTTO AND BABY LETTUCE •

Although I hardly ever use butter in cooking, I have to concede that it marries particularly well with sweet baby peas. It's almost as if the small green pearls need that luxuriant shiny coating to better melt in your mouth.

SERVES 4

40 g butter
1 tablespoon extra virgin
  olive oil
3 spring onions, thinly sliced
2–3 slices prosciutto
1 cup (250 ml) vegetable stock
salt flakes and freshly ground
  white pepper
2 cups (240 g) frozen peas
2 baby lettuce hearts,
  cut into quarters

1 Heat the butter and olive oil in a medium heavy-based frying pan over low–medium heat. Add the spring onion and prosciutto and cook for 2–3 minutes. Add the stock and a pinch of salt and bring to a simmer, then stir in the peas and lettuce and cook for 5–8 minutes or until tender. Finish with a grinding of white pepper and serve as a side dish.

• *For a vegetarian option, replace the prosciutto with parmesan or pecorino rind – just add it with the stock and continue with the recipe. Discard the rind before serving.*

MINESTRONE PRIMAVERA
◆ SPRING VEGETABLE MINESTRONE ◆

Adding pancetta or speck to this soup is a very effective way of enhancing the flavours of the spring vegetables. It's as if the precious, tender greens need a little salty boost to bring out their natural sweetness.

SERVES 4

3 tablespoons extra virgin
   olive oil, plus extra for
   drizzling
3 golden shallots, thinly sliced
½ green chilli, thinly sliced
50 g diced speck (omit for
   a vegetarian option)
1 potato, peeled and diced
salt flakes and freshly
   ground black pepper
2 artichoke hearts, cleaned
   (see page 99) and cut
   into thirds
1 litre chicken or
   vegetable stock
3 baby zucchini (courgettes),
   cut into small rounds
1 cup (220 g) baby pasta (such
   as risoni, ditalini or orzo)
1 cup (120 g) frozen peas
handful of roughly chopped
   flat-leaf parsley
freshly grated pecorino,
   to serve (omit for
   a dairy-free option)

1 Heat the olive oil in a large saucepan over medium heat. Add the shallot, chilli and speck (if using) and cook for 2–3 minutes. Add the potato and a pinch of salt and cook for 3–4 minutes, then add the artichokes and stock and another pinch or two of salt and bring to a simmer. Cook for 5 minutes, then add the zucchini.

2 Drop in the baby pasta, stir well and cook for 3–4 minutes, then add the peas and cook for 2–3 minutes or until the pasta is al dente. Turn off the heat, taste for salt and adjust according to your liking.

3 Ladle into bowls and top with parsley, freshly ground black pepper and a little extra olive oil. Crown with grated pecorino, if you like.

◆ *Barley makes a great, nutritious alternative to pasta in this dish. Simply cook it in a large saucepan of salted water for 30 minutes or until tender, then add it to the minestrone.*

A chunk of ciauscolo, a local soft cured sausage with a deliciously smoky flavour, would definitely make it onto my 'last supper' list.

Like neighbouring Molise and Abruzzo, Marche has a prolific dairy industry that produces exquisite cheeses such as pecorino marchigiano and raviggiolo. The region also specialises in truffles, which are often infused in local extra virgin olive oil.

In my past life as a classical singer I was lucky enough to perform in the gorgeous Lauro Rossi theatre in Macerata.

A TRIP TO SAN BENEDETTO DEL TRONTO

◆ ◆ · ◆ · ◆ ◆

My parents were determined to raise their children with a discerning palate. We would travel near and far on a mission to find the perfect mouthful, regardless of the steaming hot summer weather and the fact that we had no air-conditioning in the car. Mamma and Papá would pack us kids into the red Alfasud and drive as far as 150 km to the delightful seaside village of San Benedetto del Tronto for a feast of succulent prawns, golden fried calamari or everybody's favourite, polipo con patate, the local octopus and potato salad. The restaurant of choice would invariably be a kiosk on the beach, with plastic tables and chairs and a paper tablecloth the waiter would hurriedly scribble your order on. The service was lazy, the food was delightful and the memories are forever.

FRITTO MISTO

• CRISPY FRIED PRAWNS AND CALAMARI •

When making this dish, I encourage you to change the quantities and varieties of seafood according to your needs and tastes. My one condition is that you pair your fritto misto with a glass of chilled white wine. This is non-negotiable!

SERVES 4

8 uncooked tiger or
    banana prawns
500 g uncooked school prawns
2 clean calamari tubes, cut
    into 3 cm squares
1 cup (150 g) plain flour
sunflower oil, for deep-frying
salt flakes and freshly ground
    white pepper
lemon wedges, to serve

1 Remove the heads from the tiger or banana prawns. Keep them in the freezer to use for a fish reduction. Discard the heads and antennae from the school prawns.

2 Dredge the prawns and calamari in flour, then shake off the excess. Half-fill a large heavy-based frying pan with sunflower oil and heat over medium–high heat to 180°C or until a cube of bread browns in 15 seconds. Start by frying the tiger or banana prawns, turning them over to ensure even cooking. Once golden brown and crunchy, lift them out with a slotted spoon and drain on a plate lined with paper towel. Continue cooking the school prawns and calamari squares until crispy. This should take about 2–3 minutes. If your pan is not very big, you may need to cook in smaller batches.

3 Arrange the golden seafood on a platter and season with salt and pepper. Serve piping hot with lemon wedges.

• *Baby zucchini (courgettes) cut into strips make a beautiful green addition to this scrumptious dish.*

GAMBERI GRATINATI

◆ GRATINATED PRAWNS WITH LEMON AND PARSLEY ◆

This simple recipe produces a striking show-stopper of a dish that may be served as a starter or light lunch. The preparation is so fast and effortless – all that is left for you to do is proudly take it to the table and welcome all the oohs and aahs from your fellow diners with a gracious smile.

SERVES 4

1 cup (70 g) fresh
    breadcrumbs (see page 27)
1–2 handfuls of flat-leaf
    parsley leaves
pinch of salt flakes
1 long red chilli (or bird's eye,
    if you like it hot!)
½ clove garlic, peeled
1–2 small strips lemon rind
2 tablespoons extra virgin
    olive oil, plus extra
    for drizzling
12 uncooked tiger prawns
lemon cheeks, to serve

1 Turn on the grill function in your oven. Line a baking tray with baking paper.

2 Place the breadcrumbs, parsley, salt, chilli, garlic, lemon rind and olive oil in a food processor and blitz for 6–10 seconds or until combined.

3 Cut the prawns in half lengthways and top each half with a bit of the breadcrumb mixture. Press gently with your hands to ensure the coating adheres to the prawn halves. Place the prawns on the prepared tray and drizzle a little more olive oil on top, then grill for 2–3 minutes or until golden. Serve hot with lemon cheeks.

◆ *You can replace the tiger prawns with scampi, for a more extravagant version of this delightful dish.*

STROZZAPRETI con RANA PESCATRICE

• HANDMADE NOODLES WITH MONKFISH RAGÙ •

Strozzapreti (literally, priest stranglers) lends its colourful name to the various legends this hand-twisted spaghetti is associated with. Some say that gluttonous Marchigiani priests would gulp them down so quickly they'd choke. Others say that in ancient times, when the church was the big land owner of the region, housewives would labour endlessly in the kitchen, trying to satisfy the unceasing appetites of the clergymen. Jealous husbands, enraged at their abandonment, wished for the pasta to strangle the prelates. It's hard to tell how much truth there is in either legend, but they both unmistakably reflect the anticlericalism of Marchigiani!

SERVES 4

3 tablespoons extra virgin
    olive oil
2 cloves garlic, 1 whole, skin
    on, bashed with the back
    of a knife, 1 finely chopped
2 tablespoons finely chopped
    flat-leaf parsley stalks
1 × 300 g monkfish fillet
    (or ling or barramundi),
    cut into 2 cm cubes
350 g cherry tomatoes,
    cut in half
150 ml white wine
salt flakes and freshly ground
    white pepper

STROZZAPRETI

2 cups (300 g) durum wheat
    flour, specialty pasta flour
    or plain flour, plus extra
    for dusting
1 teaspoon salt flakes
220–250 ml lukewarm water
olive oil, for greasing your
    hands

1 Start by making the strozzapreti. Put the flour and salt in a large mixing bowl, make a well in the centre and slowly pour in the water, mixing as you go to incorporate the flour. Don't add all the water at once as you may not need it all, depending on the brand of flour you use; by the same token, you may need to add a little extra water if the dough is too stiff or dry. Using 100% durum wheat flour will probably require a little more liquid than plain flour or specialty pasta flour. Tip the dough onto a floured surface, oil your hands and knead for 3–4 minutes or until it comes together in a smooth ball. Add a little extra flour if it feels a bit sticky. Wrap it in plastic film and let it rest in the fridge for 30 minutes. You can make the dough a day ahead, if it's more convenient.

2 Take the dough out of the fridge. (If the dough has been refrigerated for more than 1 hour, allow it to come to room temperature before you attempt to roll it.) Dust a large wooden board with flour and roll out the dough to a thickness of 2–3 mm. Roll up the dough and cut it into 1 cm wide strips. Roll each strip with lightly oiled hands to shape your strozzapreti into 20–25 cm long strips, then dust them with a little flour and set aside.

3 Bring a large saucepan of water to the boil while you make the sauce.

4 Heat the olive oil in a large heavy-based frying pan over medium–high heat, add the garlic and parsley stalks, and cook for 1 minute or until the garlic smells fragrant and is still pale in colour. Add the fish and cherry tomatoes and cook over

• *Don't feel bad if you would like to make this dish but can't quite come to terms with the idea of homemade noodles. Dried linguine or casarecce will work just as well!*

medium heat for 1 minute. Pour in the wine and cook for 1–2 minutes or until the alcohol has evaporated, then remove from the heat. Taste for salt and pepper and adjust accordingly.

5 When the water comes to a rolling boil, drop in the noodles and cook for 2–3 minutes or until al dente. Drain, reserving 3–4 tablespoons of cooking water. Add the pasta to the sauce, with a little pasta water if it is too dry, and toss to combine. Serve hot.

CALAMARI *in* GUAZZETTO

• CALAMARI WITH TOMATOES AND WINE •

The best tip I've learnt from my chef brother about squid is not to be afraid of cooking it! Be confident, give it a few minutes over high heat and you'll be rewarded with an exquisitely tender morsel.

SERVES 4

600 g whole squid
3 tablespoons extra virgin
   olive oil
4 anchovy fillets
1 clove garlic, skin on, bashed
   with the back of a knife
2 golden shallots, thinly sliced
250 g cherry tomatoes, cut
   in half
200 ml white wine
salt flakes
roughly chopped flat-leaf
   parsley, to garnish
crusty bread, to serve

1 Start by cleaning the squid. Make sure you do this over the sink, and wear rubber gloves if you are a bit squeamish. Separate the head and tentacles from the body, then cut off the tentacles and set them aside. Discard the head and eyes. Rinse the body (the tube) under cold water to remove the innards. Pull out the thin bone and discard it. Lift the purple skin with the back of a knife and pull gently with your hands until it comes off. The wings will come off too. Now you are left with a pearl-white, clean squid tube. Cut it into 1 cm thick rings and set aside.

2 Heat the olive oil in a large heavy-based frying pan over medium–high heat, add the anchovies and stir until they melt into the oil. Add the garlic, shallot, cherry tomatoes and squid rings and cook together for 1–2 minutes. Add the wine and cook for 1–2 minutes or until the alcohol has evaporated. Taste for salt and adjust accordingly. Turn off the heat, scatter some parsley over the top and serve hot with plenty of bread.

• *I know there's a fairly large percentage of people out there who would rather set their hair on fire than eat anchovies, but let me assure you they only add a wonderful salty kick to the dish, leaving no fishy taste behind. If you are feeding non-anchovy lovers, I suggest you conveniently forget to tell them what's in the sauce. They will never know!*

POLIPO *con* PATATE
• OCTOPUS AND POTATO SALAD •

Mamma makes a mean octopus and potato salad, a beloved combination in the heart of most Italians. If cooking this intriguing-looking cephalopod scares you, allow me to share her method, which is brilliant in its simplicity. Forget about beating the creature with a meat mallet, plunging it into boiling water three times while praying to the Madonna, or boiling it with a cork. Mamma was told by her local fishmonger that the one trick to ensure succulent flesh is to simply stew the octopus in a little extra virgin olive oil, a few bay leaves and a splash of wine, until the mollusc surrenders to its cooking nectar and is so tender you don't need a knife to cut it. Matched with steamed potatoes, fresh parsley and a drizzle of the cooking juices, it speaks of Italian summer in each and every mouthful.

SERVES 4

1–1.5 kg octopus
100 ml white wine
2 tablespoons extra virgin olive oil, plus extra for drizzling
1–2 bay leaves
3–4 white peppercorns
3–4 medium potatoes, peeled
salt flakes and freshly ground white pepper
roughly chopped flat-leaf parsley, to garnish
crusty bread, to serve (optional)

1 Place the octopus in a large heavy-based saucepan or wok and add the wine, olive oil, bay leaves and peppercorns. Bring to a simmer, then reduce the heat to low, cover with a fitted lid and gently poach for 60–70 minutes or until fork tender. Set aside to cool completely in the pan.

2 Meanwhile, place the potatoes in a large saucepan of cold salted water. Bring to the boil, then reduce the heat and simmer for 30–35 minutes or until cooked through. Drain and allow to cool for 10–15 minutes.

3 Take the octopus out of the pan, reserving the poaching liquid, and set it on a board to clean. Cut off the head, then flip it inside out and pull out the innards. Rinse under cold water to remove any grit, if necessary. Cut the body in half lengthways, then push your thumbs through the middle to ease out the beak. Discard. Pull off the skin using your fingers or by rubbing the tentacles with a tea towel.

4 To assemble the dish, cut the octopus and potatoes into bite-sized chunks and arrange in a bowl. Drizzle with a little extra olive oil and 2–3 tablespoons of the reserved poaching liquid, season with salt and pepper, and scatter with parsley. Enjoy with crusty bread (if using) as a stunning antipasto or light lunch.

• *When shopping for octopus, make sure you choose one that has not been frozen and then thawed, to ensure great tenderness once cooked.*

San Benedetto del Tronto

Practising my dunking action with the sweet offerings of Osteria dei Pilgiapochi.

Giuseppe and me at
Osteria dei Pilgiapochi, Macerata

PATATE ARROSTO con ALLORO e GUANCIALE

• ROAST POTATOES WITH BAY LEAVES AND CURED PORK CHEEK •

I don't think I'm alone here when I confess that I go to the trouble of making a Sunday roast purely so that I can indulge in crisp, golden potatoes. Yes, I love roast lamb, beef and chicken, but only if they come with a generous side of these golden delights. Central Italy is blessed with a holy combination of good soil, water and a miracle from the Madonna thrown in for good measure – the perfect environment for growing this mighty tuber. And for those friends of mine (you know who you are) whose carb-free diets have robbed them of this culinary pleasure, let me tell you that you are also missing out on a great source of potassium, fibre, vitamin C, iron and zinc!

SERVES 4

1 kg red potatoes (desiree or pontiac), well washed
200 g guanciale (cured pork cheek – replace with pancetta or speck if preferred), cut into cubes
100 ml extra virgin olive oil
3–4 cloves garlic, skin on, bashed with the back of a knife
salt flakes
3–4 bay leaves

1 Place the potatoes in a large saucepan of cold salted water. Bring to the boil and cook for 20–25 minutes or until the potatoes are soft and the skin is starting to crack. Drain the potatoes in a colander and shake off the excess liquid. This will rough up the edges and encourage the potatoes to break into chunks. Allow the moisture from the potatoes to evaporate slightly.

2 Meanwhile, preheat your oven to 220°C (200°C fan-forced).

3 While the oven is heating up, place a large heavy-based, ovenproof frying pan over high heat. Drop in the guanciale with 1 tablespoon of the olive oil, then reduce the heat to low–medium and cook for 5–10 minutes or until the pork has rendered its fat and crisped up nicely. Remove the guanciale with a slotted spoon and set aside.

4 Add the garlic and potatoes to the pan with the remaining oil, season with salt and cook over medium–high heat for 3–4 minutes. Add the bay leaves and place the pan in the oven. Reduce the temperature to 200°C (180°C fan-forced) and roast for 35–40 minutes or until golden and crisp. Return the guanciale to the pan and serve hot as a side dish or on its own, with greens.

• *In the unlikely event of leftovers, slice the potatoes thinly and add them to the egg mixture for your next frittata (see page 107).*

CONIGLIO
in PORCHETTA
◆ ROLLED DEBONED RABBIT ◆

To cook meat 'in porchetta' is to cook it as if it were a deboned pig (porco) rolled with a herb and meat stuffing. In the Marche region they like to take the pork out of the porchetta and replace it with something smaller, easier to roll and equally tasty: rabbit. My most heartfelt advice is to ask your butcher to debone the rabbit for you. Beg, if necessary – I did! Don't attempt to do it yourself unless you have extremely nimble hands and a natural gift for highly skilled butchery.

SERVES 4

1 kg deboned rabbit
salt flakes and freshly ground
    black pepper
3 tablespoons extra virgin
    olive oil
200 ml white wine

STUFFING
3 tablespoons extra virgin
    olive oil
1 brown onion, roughly
    chopped
1 carrot, roughly chopped
1 celery stick, roughly
    chopped
2–3 sprigs thyme
30 g smoked pancetta or
    speck, diced
2 teaspoons fennel seeds
the rabbit livers (ask your
    butcher to reserve them
    for you)
250 g pork sausage meat,
    removed from its casing
salt flakes
150 ml white wine

1   To make the stuffing, heat the olive oil in a large frying pan over medium heat, add the onion, carrot, celery and thyme and cook for 2–3 minutes or until softened. Add the pancetta or speck and cook together until most of the fat has rendered and the meat is starting to turn crispy. Add the fennel seeds, livers and sausage meat and brown well for 3–4 minutes, breaking up the sausage meat with a wooden spoon. Season with a pinch of salt. Pour in the wine and cook over medium–high heat for 2–3 minutes or until the alcohol has evaporated. Reduce the heat to low and cook for a further 15–20 minutes or until the meat is cooked through. Remove from the heat and allow to cool completely. Discard the thyme sprigs. If you like, you can make the stuffing the day before and rest it in the fridge, wrapped in plastic film.

2   To assemble the dish, place the deboned rabbit on a large wooden board and season it with salt and pepper. Spoon the cold stuffing down the centre, then tie the rabbit securely with kitchen string to enclose the stuffing.

3   Heat the olive oil in a large flameproof casserole dish over medium–high heat and brown the stuffed rabbit on all sides, then pour in the wine and cook for 2–3 minutes or until the alcohol has evaporated. Reduce the heat to low and cook, covered, for 45–50 minutes, turning the rabbit once, and basting occasionally with the pan juices.

4   Remove the casserole dish from the heat and rest the rabbit in its juices for 20 minutes before carving. This is delicious with any vegetable dish, but I particularly enjoy it with sautéed artichokes (see page 102) or broccolini cooked with chilli and garlic (see page 232).

POLLO in POTACCHIO

• BRAISED CHICKEN MARYLANDS WITH WINE AND TOMATOES •

The very intriguing sounding 'pollo in potacchio' can be loosely translated as 'braised chicken in a pot'. But this seems to strip this wondrous dish of its beauty! Here is a simple but infallible marriage of a few humble ingredients. Every town, village and hamlet in the Marche area has a variation on this recipe, but what they all share is a strong sense of regional pride and, most importantly, glorious flavours.

SERVES 4

4 tablespoons extra virgin
    olive oil
4 cloves garlic, skin on,
    bashed with the back
    of a knife
2–3 sprigs rosemary
handful of oregano leaves
4 chicken marylands
    (leg and thigh portions),
    excess fat removed
200 ml white wine
salt flakes
250 g cherry tomatoes,
    some kept whole,
    some cut in half
crusty bread, to serve

1 Preheat your oven to 220°C (200°C fan-forced).

2 Heat the olive oil in a large ovenproof frying pan or flameproof casserole dish over medium–high heat. Add the garlic and herbs and cook for 1–2 minutes, then add the chicken and cook for 10–12 minutes on each side. Deglaze the pan with the white wine and simmer for 1–2 minutes to allow the alcohol to evaporate, then season with salt.

3 Scatter over the cherry tomatoes, then put the pan or dish in the oven for 20–25 minutes to finish cooking the chicken. Towards the end of the cooking time, turn on the grill function to give it a golden, scorched look.

4 Serve hot or warm, with plenty of bread to mop up that heavenly, wine-infused sauce.

◆ *Pollo in potacchio will keep well in the fridge for up to a day. As it cools the sauce will firm up, so make sure you reheat it thoroughly to allow it to return to its glorious, liquid state.*

POLLO alla BOSCAIOLA

• WOODSMAN'S CHICKEN •

What could go wrong when you are roasting succulent chicken thighs with a bunch of aromatic ingredients such as olive oil, white wine, pancetta and porcini mushrooms? That's right, nothing! This is because, in the tradition of Italian rustic cuisine, your only job as a cook is to trust your ingredients, know what's in season and bring them together with a bit of common sense and love. I tasted this dish in the gorgeous town of Recanati, and the chef crowned it with a healthy shaving of local black truffle. I've replaced this rather extravagant ingredient with mushrooms – giving the dish a solid flavour burst that won't empty your pockets.

SERVES 4–6

3 potatoes, peeled and cut into 5 mm thick slices

3–4 tablespoons extra virgin olive oil, plus extra for greasing

8 chicken thigh fillets

salt flakes and freshly ground black pepper

4 cloves garlic, skin on, bashed with the back of a knife

150 ml white wine

a few sprigs thyme

4–5 thin slices smoked pancetta or streaky bacon

1 cup (about 50 g) mixed mushrooms (field, portobello, porcini – anything but button mushrooms!), cleaned and sliced

1 Preheat your oven to 220°C (200°C fan-forced).

2 Parboil the potato slices in a saucepan of salted boiling water for 2–3 minutes. Drain carefully, trying not to break up the pieces, and set aside.

3 Grease a medium baking dish with olive oil. Arrange half the potato slices over the base of the dish. Season the chicken thighs with salt and pepper, then place them over the potato. Arrange the remaining potato over the chicken, along with the garlic cloves. Drizzle the olive oil and wine on top, scatter over the thyme sprigs and season with a little extra salt. Cover the dish with foil and bake for 15 minutes.

4 Remove the foil and arrange the pancetta or bacon slices over the chicken and potato. Scatter the mushroom over the top, then bake, uncovered, for a further 20 minutes. Turn on the grill function in your oven towards the end of the cooking time to encourage the pancetta to crisp up and the chicken to develop a light, healthy tan. Serve hot!

• *Pollo alla boscaiola is divine accompanied by bread or soft polenta to mop up those precious wine, chicken and mushroom juices. To make soft polenta, pour 3 litres water into a large saucepan, salt well and bring to a simmer. Slowly rain in 500 g coarse polenta, whisking constantly to prevent any lumps forming. Reduce the heat to low and cook for 35–40 minutes, stirring frequently, always in the same direction (strange as it may sound). You know it's cooked when it feels luscious and silky and not grainy. Season to taste with salt.*

CORATELLA di AGNELLO

• SAUTÉED LAMB OFFAL •

Coratella is the Italian word for lamb's pluck, a cluster of organs (lungs, liver and heart) that normally comes connected to the oesophagus. Yes, I will concede this dish is not for the faint-hearted, but let me assure you that coratella is a triumph of texture and flavour, where the creamy, delicate liver, soft, pillowy lungs and wholesome, rich hearts are happily brought together with softened brown onion, extra virgin olive oil and fresh herbs. Those brave enough to attempt this recipe will be faced with the challenge of sourcing the offal, quite possibly not one of the best sellers at the local supermarket. Persistence, and perhaps engaging in mild flirtation with your butcher, should do the trick. And while you're at it, ask him to give you a hand easing the lungs away from the membrane, a finicky job I never really enjoy.

Coratella can be served as a main course, accompanied by roasted artichokes and potatoes, but in many agriturismi (see Note) around Marche it is offered with crusty bread as part of an antipasto spread.

~~~~~~~~~~~~~~~~~~~~~~~~~~~~~ SERVES 4 ~~~~~~~~~~~~~~~~~~~~~~~~~~~~~

500 g coratella (ask your butcher for lamb's pluck)
100 ml extra virgin olive oil
1 brown onion, thinly sliced
4–5 sage leaves
2–3 sprigs marjoram
2–3 sprigs thyme
salt flakes
lemon cheeks and potato chips (optional; see Note), to serve

1 Prepare the coratella by pulling the lungs away from the membrane (or ask you butcher to do this for you). Cut the lungs, hearts and livers into small, even-sized pieces.

2 Heat the olive oil in a medium heavy-based frying pan over low–medium heat. Add the onion, herbs and a pinch of salt and cook for 2–3 minutes or until the onion starts to soften. Add the lungs. Increase the heat to medium and cook for 10–15 minutes or until you hear a sound similar to a high-pitched whistle. Add the hearts and cook for 1–2 minutes, then add the livers and cook for a further 1–2 minutes.

3 Remove the pan from the heat, season with a pinch of salt and a squeeze of lemon juice, and serve hot, with potato chips, if liked.

~~~~~~

- *Agriturismi are farmhouses set up as restaurants that serve regional food prepared with local ingredients, often grown or bred onsite. They are rustic and simple, and offer a true insight into the Italian tradition of cucina povera (peasant cooking).*
- *To make potato chips, peel 2 medium potatoes and cut them into 2–3 mm thick slices. Deep-fry them in olive oil for 4–5 minutes or until golden. Drain on paper towel and serve hot, seasoned with salt.*

VINCISGRASSI

• LASAGNE MARCHE STYLE •

Vincisgrassi is the Marchigiano cousin to the famous lasagne from the neighbouring Emilia Romagna region. The story goes that the dish was first made to impress an Austrian general called Windisch Graetz, whose army passed through the Marche region in 1799. The combination of freshly made pasta and braised meats slow-baked in the oven certainly proved to be to the general's liking, and the recipe continues to be one of Italy's most loved pasta dishes, ever present at the Italian festive table – whatever you wish to call it and whomever you wish to impress!

My father's aunt Dina, who was from these parts, passed on her trick for making a luxurious meat sauce, ready to coat the silky layers of pasta: a good drop of vin santo, a sweet, perfumed wine from central Italy. *Pictured page 64.*

SERVES 6–8

Recanati, Marche

1 quantity egg pasta dough
made with 4 eggs and
2⅔ cups (400 g) type '00'
flour (see page 128), rolled
into 3 mm thick sheets
butter, for greasing and
for baking
2½ cups (200 g) freshly
grated parmigiano
300 g bocconcini, well
drained, torn

RAGÙ
4 tablespoons extra virgin
olive oil
1 brown onion, roughly
chopped
1 carrot, roughly chopped
1 celery stick, roughly chopped
400 g beef mince
100 g chicken livers, sinew
removed with a paring knife
300 g pork sausage meat,
removed from its casing
salt flakes and freshly ground
black pepper
100 ml vin santo (or other sweet
wine, such as Marsala)
2 × 400 g tins tomatoes
or 800 ml passata
1–2 bay leaves

BÉCHAMEL SAUCE
60 g butter
60 g plain flour
1 litre milk
pinch of salt flakes
pinch of grated nutmeg

1 To make the ragù, heat the olive oil in a large frying pan over medium heat, add the onion, carrot and celery and cook for 2–3 minutes or until softened. Add the beef, livers and sausage meat and brown over high heat for 3–4 minutes. (If your pan is too small, brown the meat in batches so that it doesn't stew.) Season with a pinch of salt, then pour in the vin santo and cook over high heat for 2–3 minutes to allow the alcohol to evaporate. Add the tomatoes or passata and bay leaves and bring to a simmer, then reduce the heat to low and cook, covered, for 3–4 hours or until rich and flavoursome. After that time, taste it and season accordingly with salt and pepper.

2 To make the béchamel sauce, melt the butter in a small saucepan over low–medium heat, add the flour and cook for 1–2 minutes. Slowly pour in the milk and whisk vigorously to remove any lumps. Bring to a simmer and cook, stirring with a wooden spoon, for 6–8 minutes. Season with salt and nutmeg and set aside.

3 Preheat your oven to 200°C (180°C fan-forced).

4 Cut the rolled pasta into sheets to fit your lasagne dish. Blanch the pasta sheets in a large saucepan of salted boiling water for 1 minute. Drain on clean tea towels, without overlapping them.

5 To assemble, grease a 30 cm × 45 cm baking dish with the butter. Spread a ladleful of béchamel on the base, and top with a layer of lasagne. Add a layer of ragù and béchamel, and sprinkle with a little parmigiano and bocconcini. Repeat with the remaining ingredients to create 3–4 layers. Finish with a ladle each of béchamel and ragù and a final dusting of parmigiano. Scatter over a few small dots of butter, then cover with foil and bake for 20 minutes. Remove the foil and bake for a further 10–15 minutes or until golden. Remove from the oven and cover with foil, then leave to rest for 30 minutes before serving.

• *You can assemble the dish a day ahead and leave it in the fridge, covered in foil. When you are ready to cook it, put the baking dish (still covered in foil) in the preheated oven and bake as instructed.*

◄ LASAGNE MARCHE STYLE (see page 62)

The name of this region derives from the word 'march' (frontier). When the marches of Ancona, Camerino and Fermo were formed, sometime around the 11th century, the region became known in Italy as Le Marche (The Marches).

TORTA ALL'OLIO *e* ALBICOCCHE

• APRICOT AND OLIVE OIL CAKE •

Olive oil is commonly used instead of butter in central and southern Italy, even in the baking of cakes and sweet pastries. It imparts a subtle touch of savoury, but also adds lightness to cake batters. However, the real secret to the ineffable fluffiness of this cake is that the sugar is first dissolved in warm milk and infused with lemon and vanilla. The apricots add a welcome touch of tangy tartness, making this cake impossible to resist for morning or afternoon tea.

SERVES 8

170 g caster sugar
230 ml milk
finely grated zest of 1 lemon
1 vanilla bean, split and
    seeds scraped
100 ml extra virgin olive oil
3 teaspoons mistrà or
    sambuca (optional;
    see Note)
2 eggs, lightly beaten
1⅓ cups (200 g) self-raising
    flour
½ teaspoon bicarbonate
    of soda
7–8 apricots, cut into quarters
flaked almonds, for sprinkling
fresh ricotta and honey,
    to serve (optional)

1 Preheat your oven to 180°C (160°C fan-forced). Grease and flour a 27 cm × 21 cm rectangular or 21 cm square cake tin (or line it with baking paper).

2 Place the sugar, milk and lemon zest in a medium saucepan over low heat and cook for 3–4 minutes, stirring regularly, until the sugar has dissolved. Do not let the milk come to the boil. Turn off the heat and stir in the vanilla seeds, olive oil and liqueur (if using), then let the mixture cool for 5–10 minutes.

3 Add the beaten egg, flour and bicarbonate of soda and whisk to form a smooth batter. Pour the batter into the prepared tin and arrange the apricot quarters on top any way you like. Sprinkle with the flaked almonds and bake for 30–35 minutes or until pale golden and a skewer inserted into the middle of the cake comes out clean. Cool in the tin for a few minutes, then turn out onto a wire rack and cool at room temperature for 1 hour before cutting. Serve just as it is or with honey-drizzled ricotta.

- *Mistrà is an aniseed-scented liqueur often enjoyed in Marche. For an alcohol-free version, replace the liqueur with milk.*
- *If you are using very small apricots, they may plummet to the bottom of the tin during baking. To avoid this, make a double layer of apricot quarters.*

CIAMBELLONE di LIMONE e RICOTTA

◆ LEMON AND RICOTTA RING CAKE ◆

Quite simply, this is the most perfect dunking cake. And if you have travelled around Italy you will know that we love nothing more than dunking something sweet into our morning coffee, afternoon hot chocolate or evening red wine or amaro. Ciambellone, a doughnut-shaped cake, is the offspring of sponge cake and madeira cake – moist and light, but with some texture. Although most regions of Italy have a much-loved version, Marche takes the crown when it comes to how vigorously the locals claim to be the rightful birth parents of this cake. This is my version, inspired by premium local produce, so abundant in this region. I warn you now that this is arguably the easiest cake recipe ever, and this disarming simplicity can become perilously addictive . . .

SERVES 8

3 eggs

200 g caster sugar, plus extra for dusting

4 tablespoons extra virgin olive oil

170 g fresh full-cream ricotta, well drained

210 g self-raising flour, sifted

70 g almond meal

finely grated zest of 2 lemons

juice of 1 lemon

1 teaspoon vanilla paste or extract (or the seeds scraped from ½ vanilla bean)

1 tablespoon amaretto (optional; see Note)

mascarpone or honeyed ricotta, to serve (optional)

1 Preheat the oven to 170°C (150°C fan-forced). Butter and flour a Bundt tin.

2 In a large bowl, beat the eggs with the sugar until pale and creamy. Add the olive oil and ricotta and mix until smooth. Gently fold in the flour and almond meal, then add the lemon zest and juice, vanilla and amaretto (if using).

3 Pour the batter into the prepared tin and bake for 35–40 minutes or until a skewer inserted into the middle of the cake comes out clean. Allow to cool completely in the tin before turning out onto a plate. Dust with sugar and serve as it is or with a dollop of mascarpone or honeyed ricotta.

◆ *Give the amaretto a miss for an alcohol-free option.*

TOZZETTI

• ALMOND AND LEMON BISCOTTI •

Tozzetti, also known as cantuccini, are Italy's best-loved cookies. They serve many useful purposes: you can dunk them in your morning coffee, in your afternoon gelato, and in your evening vin santo. They are also practically fat-free. The fact that they make up for this with a plentiful supply of sugar make these biscotti an Italian confectionery marvel.

MAKES ABOUT 30

2 eggs
3 egg yolks
350 g caster sugar
1 teaspoon vanilla paste
    or extract
3 cups (450 g) self-raising
    flour, sifted
1 tablespoon melted butter
pinch of salt flakes
finely grated zest of 2 lemons
1¼ cups (200 g) natural
    almonds

1 Preheat your oven to 190°C (170°C fan-forced) and line a large baking tray with baking paper.

2 Place the eggs, egg yolks, sugar and vanilla in a mixing bowl and beat until pale and creamy. Add the flour, butter, salt and lemon zest and then the nuts. Shape the dough with floured hands to form two logs. Place the logs on the prepared tray, spaced apart to allow for spreading, and bake for 25–30 minutes or until well risen and pale golden.

3 Remove from the oven and cool at room temperature for 3–5 minutes, then cut them on an angle into 1–1.5 cm thick slices. Make sure you use a very sharp serrated knife to ensure neat slices. You will notice that the inside of the biscuits are still a little wet – this is fine.

4 Arrange the slices on the lined tray and return to the oven for 5 minutes. Turn them over and toast for a further 5 minutes or until crisp and golden. Cool at room temperature, then serve with gelato, coffee or your favourite dessert wine. Any leftover tozzetti will keep in an airtight container for up to 2 weeks.

• *For a gluttonous twist on this classic, replace the almonds with hazelnuts and the lemon zest with chocolate chips.*

Donkeys in Villetta Barrea, Abruzzo

ABRUZZO

— STRONG AND GENTLE —

Although I was born and raised in Milan, my food loyalty mostly lies within the mountains and valleys of Abruzzo, a stunning and fertile region just a few hours east of Rome, where Mamma's family is from. I grew up feeling more Abruzzese than Milanese, partly because of the breathtaking beauty of the ancient land which is still inhabited by wolves, eagles and bears, but mostly for the spirit of its inhabitants and their honest, robust cuisine built around the superb local ingredients. 🦎

An old trabocco, Fossacesia

Despite its produce attaining international fame, the area remains largely undiscovered by foreign tourism, something I am both content with and dissatisfied by! The proud Abruzzese woman in me longs to keep this treasure safe from prying eyes, from flocks of visitors falling in love with its exquisite countryside and claiming it as their own.

If you travel through the more pastoral areas of Abruzzo, you will quickly learn that locals are fairly guarded when it comes to outsiders. Walking around a village as a foreigner (think flip flops, blond hair and blue eyes – well, picture my Aussie husband!) can be rather confronting. Conversations come to an abrupt stop, as the old ladies wrapped in black scarves standing at their thresholds stare intently at the stranger, speculating about his secret motives. A frown forms across their wrinkled foreheads: 'Chi e' chiss? E mo che vo'?' (And who is this stranger? What is he after?)

In this, not much has changed since the time of the Sanniti, the ancient tribe that settled this territory, who fiercely tried to guard it against the Roman invaders. In the stony, dark Abruzzese gaze, you can still discern this pride and yes, suspicion. And you sense it's something you really don't want to mess with …

Yet paradoxically the Abruzzesi can also be the most gentle and generous people you will ever encounter. Once you break through those outer barriers (a glass or two of Centerbe, the throat-scorching local digestivo, can speed up this process) and gain some trust, you will experience a lively and embracing conviviality, and you will know that it is genuine.

Whether they are from the rugged mountains or the Adriatic coast, the people of Abruzzo will invariably open their doors to you. And if you are really charming, they'll share their stories with you over thick slices of homemade cheese and salami and small almond pastries, and perhaps a glass or two of Trebbiano. Primo Levi, one of Italy's most admired writers, concisely described the region of Abruzzo as 'forte e gentile' (strong and gentle), characteristics which are manifest to this day in the quiet dignity of its inhabitants.

This is why that other side of me – the Australian woman campaigning for authentic Italian food – fervently wants to share such glorious wealth with you all. Abruzzo is a treasure trove of wonders, with its varied terrain ranging from the soft-sand beaches of the Adriatic coast and verdant hills of the National Park, to the snowy mountain peaks and the southernmost European glacier, the Calderone. Naturally, each diverse landscape has a profusion of local folklore and outstanding cuisines, from fiadone, the regional ricotta cheesecake (see page 181) and sagne e fasciul', a robust bean soup (see page 148), to wholesome lamb dishes and our beloved pasta. Whether it is dried or freshly made, the pasta dishes of Abruzzo are ubiquitous and come in an enormous variety. It makes perfect sense that three of the best pasta makers in Italy – De Cecco, Cocco and Delverde – all have their factories in Fara San Martino, a splendid village just a short drive away from Mamma's birthplace. Ask her why that pasta is so special and she'll say it's because it's made with three ingredients no money can buy: crisp, clean water from the mountain springs, a ventilated climate (perfect for pasta drying), and a healthy sense of pride.

And while I'm talking about pride, I'm so delighted to have the opportunity to introduce you to my family village, Torricella Peligna – my safe haven, my cultural inheritance. This is where Mamma and her sister Rita were born and raised until the mid-fifties when, out of financial necessity, their family like so many post-war families had to relocate to Milan.

Torricella is a small, rural village in the province of Chieti, perched 901 metres above sea level. Spend a little time in Torricella, and you will find yourself seduced by local habits . . . spending lazy mornings reading the papers or playing burraco (a popular card game) in the shade of the pineta (pine forest), or meeting locals at the Penna Nera bar, where Adamo and Marziale will regale you with their hilarious tales while the beaming Angiolina mixes up Campari and soda. (By the way, Adamo makes a mean iced coffee too – don't miss it!)

The corso (main street) of Torricella stretches from the pineta right up to the old stone church. A long flight of rocky steps will take you up to the square and the war memorial, La Torre. From this vantage point, the view up to Majella Mountain is simply astonishing. On clear days the vista stretches as far as the blue line of the Adriatic. If you look in the direction of Palena you will spot the Gigante che Dorme (the sleeping giant), a mountain peak in the form of a huge, resting man. My personal memories of La Torre are far from bucolic though: this is where my cousins, my friends and I used to come after hours, after a quick trip to the local bakery. Equipped with freshly baked goods, guitars and beer we'd spend our summer nights singing, playing spin the bottle and sharing those first, awkward kisses . . .

On the streets that run perpendicular to the corso are clusters of small, charming houses built with rocks from the Majella and decorated with elaborate wrought-iron work. As so often happens, these beauties are mixed up with the occasional post-war eyesores which were built in a hurry, with no sense of preserving the local artisanal traditions.

A left turn just before the steep slope leading up to the church will take you all the way down the contrada di Sant'Antonio, where my parents recently gave new life to a derelict farmhouse situated on a block of land rich with wild berries, apricot and fig trees. Ambling down the dirt road that leads to the sanctuary of Madonna delle Rose (Our Lady of the Roses) is a heart-warming experience with beautiful glimpses over the valleys below. Be sure to bring along a basket to collect the wild blackberries on the way. In late August, these plump, sun-soaked berries are bursting with sweet, purple nectar, perfect to eat on the spot or to turn into jam.

This is the village that I return to when I need to reconnect with life at its simplest. No complications, no hurry, no social media. Time slows. And I do too. As they say here, 'chian chian, dolc dolc' (go slow, and go sweet). ✳

With my Miro

Roccascalegna, a medieval village a short drive from Mamma's village, is famous for its stunning castle sitting on a steep rock of limestone. Legend has it that in the 1600s it was the dwelling of the evil Baron Corvo de Corvis, a nobleman who terrorised the people of Roccascalegna. Perhaps his worst form of torture was the introduction of the 'Jus primae noctis' (the right for the first night), which forced newlywed brides to lie with him on their wedding night, before they could be with their grooms. One winter's night, in an act of rebellious desperation, a young bride stabbed the Baron in the heart. Moments before he passed, the dying man stamped his blood-soaked hand on the wall, leaving a scarlet stain that could not be wiped away. They say it remained visible until 1940, when the wall fell in ruin. I am surprised Hollywood has not made a movie out of this tale. Johnny Depp would make a fine Baron!

Signor Domenico, holding his wife's freshly baked bread (Pescocostanzo)

Signora Maria, from Hotel il Pescatore in Villetta Barrea, gave us a pasta-making masterclass. She was so fast our photographer Carla could hardly keep up with her!

PIZZA SCIMA

• WHITE WINE UNLEAVENED BREAD •

Pizza scima is a traditional unleavened Abruzzese bread. It literally means 'silly pizza', as it lacks yeast, but there is nothing silly about it – its value lies in the tradition it carries. Pizza scima is said to have been around in the ancient hamlets of Gessopalena, Torricella and Roccascalegna since the 15th century and used to be a great household staple, as most of the original ingredients were easy to come by. These days it is still available in bakeries around Abruzzo, but nothing can beat the homemade version my neighbour Matilde makes. When I asked Matilde for her recipe, she kindly wrote it down for me, but I know the local villagers far too well to trust a recipe they write . . . They may indeed list all the right ingredients, but I had to see for myself the way she mixed them together and how she kneaded the dough, and exactly what she meant by 'a small glass of oil'.

This exquisite bread only requires six ingredients, yet this humble combination provides a flaky, pastry-like bread that crumbles in your mouth as you devour it with morsels of homemade salami, cheese and olives, all happily washed down with a drop of Montepulciano.

SERVES 6

4 cups (600 g) type '00' flour
100 ml extra virgin olive oil
4 tablespoons white wine
tip of a teaspoon of
　　bicarbonate of soda
2 tablespoons salt flakes
150–200 ml sparkling water

1　Preheat your oven to 220°C (200°C fan-forced).

2　Place the flour on a board or in a large bowl and make a well in the centre. Add the olive oil, wine, bicarbonate of soda and salt and mix with a wooden spoon to encourage the dough to come together. Add the sparkling water, a little at a time, to form a soft dough. Start by adding 150 ml, then see if you need to add the rest.

3　Knead the dough on a floured surface for a few minutes, then flatten it out with a rolling pin to a thickness of about 2 cm. Put the dough on an oiled baking tray and score it with a serrated knife to create a criss-cross pattern. Bake for 30–35 minutes, or until golden and the scent of wine and olive oil is starting to make you salivate in anticipation.

* *When Signora Matilde taught me her recipe, she let me in on another kitchen secret: it is better to perform the act of cooking with a glass of chilled martini and lemon in hand. I have not abandoned the habit since!*

Signora Crispina at work in her kitchen.

The wide green pastures make this land the perfect environment for breeding sheep and goats. The ancient practice of transhumance, the migration of herds from the highlands to the lowlands, still takes place twice a year.

PIZZELLE SALATE
con VINO

• SAVOURY WHITE WINE AND OLIVE OIL WAFFLES •

Pizzelle, or ferratelle, are typical of both Abruzzo and Molise. They are the Italian equivalent of waffles, and come in both sweet and savoury incarnations. The recipes vary from village to village, and hardly any come with a written method. It's one of those gastronomic wonders that is explained to you by the ladies who still make them as 'a bit of this, a bit of that, mix and cook until it's ready'. Mamma's way, which produces a delightfully crisp morsel that cries out to be paired with olives, slices of salami and chunks of pecorino, uses a wine tumbler as its unit of measurement: '1 glass of wine, 1 glass of oil, salt and pepper and flour . . . just enough!'

Here is her method translated into more intelligible cooking instructions.

MAKES 10

¾ cup (185 ml) extra virgin olive oil
2½ tablespoons water
¾ cup (185 ml) white wine
1⅓ cups (200 g) plain flour
salt flakes and freshly ground white pepper
cold cuts of meat and cheese and/or olives, to serve

1 Mix together the olive oil, water and wine in a large mixing bowl. Gradually add the flour, whisking well to form a smooth batter similar in texture to a pancake batter, only slightly thicker. You will find that sometimes you need more or less flour to achieve a perfect result. This is because all flours vary slightly, even within the same brand. Let your instinct guide you – you won't fail. Season the batter with salt and pepper.

2 Heat a pizzelle, waffle or jaffle camping iron. Grease it with butter or, as my nonna used to do, with the fat from sliced prosciutto.

3 Put 2 tablespoons batter in the mould, close the lid and cook until golden and the scent of wine and olive oil permeates the room. If using a pizzelle iron or a jaffle camping iron, turn it over halfway through to ensure even cooking.

4 Serve warm with salami, pecorino, olives or whatever suits your palate.

• *Pizzelle salate are best served warm, which is lucky as leftovers are really unlikely to occur . . .*

PALLOTTE CACIO e OVO

• STALE BREAD AND PECORINO DUMPLINGS •

The literal translation for this traditional dish from my mother's village is 'balls with pecorino and egg' . . . it doesn't sound quite as evocative in English! But don't let the name fool you. Every mamma and nonna in Torricella Peligna has a treasured recipe for this humble dish featuring stale bread, and they all believe themselves to be the keeper of the best version. I am no exception, having inherited Great Aunt Italina's method, which involves leaving a chunk of capsicum to stew in the sauce, adding a touch of peppery robustness to this magnificent peasant meal.

SERVES 4

3 tablespoons extra virgin
   olive oil
2 spring onions, roughly chopped
1 clove garlic, skin on, bashed
   with the back of a knife,
   1 finely chopped
1 small celery stick, finely
   chopped
¼ green capsicum (pepper)
   in 1 piece
2 × 400 g tins tomatoes
200 ml water
salt flakes and freshly ground
   black pepper
basil leaves, to garnish

DUMPLINGS
200 g day-old Italian bread
1 cup (250 ml) milk
2 cups (160 g) finely grated
   pecorino
1 egg and 1 egg yolk,
   lightly beaten
3 tablespoons roughly
   chopped flat-leaf parsley
3 tablespoons roughly
   chopped basil
salt flakes and freshly ground
   black pepper
olive oil, for deep-frying

1 To make the dumplings, remove the crusts from the bread and cut it into chunks. Soak it in the milk for 20 minutes or until soft. Squeeze out any excess liquid then, using your hands, break down the bread to a pulp. Add the pecorino, egg and herbs and mix to form a sticky batter. This stickiness will ensure the softness of your dumplings. Season to taste with salt and pepper, then rest in the fridge for 20 minutes.

2 Meanwhile, heat the extra virgin olive oil in a frying pan over medium–high heat. Add the spring onion, garlic, celery and capsicum and cook, stirring, for 3–4 minutes or until fragrant. Add the tomatoes and water, season with salt and bring to a simmer. Reduce the heat to low and cook gently for 20 minutes or until reduced slightly.

3 To cook the dumplings, half-fill a saucepan with olive oil and heat over medium–high heat to 180°C or until a cube of bread browns in 15 seconds. With wet hands, shape the dumpling mixture into 5 cm balls. Add the dumplings to the oil in batches and cook for 3–4 minutes or until golden and cooked through. Remove with a slotted spoon and drain on a plate lined with paper towel.

4 Add the cooked dumplings to the tomato sauce, cover with the lid and stand, off the heat, for at least 1 hour before serving to allow the flavours to mingle and the dumplings to soak up the sauce. Reheat if you like or serve warm, garnished with basil.

• *This dish tastes even better the next day – if you have any leftovers, that is.*

Abruzzo is the birthplace of very many notable people, such as composer Vincenzo Bellini (senior), poet Ovid, writer Gabriele D'Annunzio, Corradino D'Ascanio (the inventor of the Vespa) and philosopher Benedetto Croce. Interestingly, Nonno Domenico, whose surname was Croce, used to boast that we were his descendants. Naturally, I disgraced the family when my philosophy teacher in high school failed me!

MAMMA AND PAPÀ'S ARTICHOKE RECIPES

◆ ◆ ◇ ◆ ◇ ◆ ◆

Seasonality has always been paramount in Mamma's kitchen. Every Saturday morning, she and Papà would pack the three of us into the car and cart us around various markets to source the best produce at reasonable prices. They stoically endured our grumpy moods and sibling tiffs in the name of the greater good: the produce! More often than not, arriving at their preferred stall as the vendors were ready to pack up for the day meant that we'd go home with boxes of heavily discounted fruit and vegetables, ready to reach their true potential under Mamma's expert hands. Artichokes have always been a favoured choice in springtime. (Yes, I'll admit they can be a bit finicky to prepare, but they are well worth the effort.) As soon as we got home from the market, we kids would be quickly fed a panino and put in front of re-runs of *Pippi Longstocking*, leaving Mamma and Papà free to wrangle the thorny thistles with nimble hands at rapid speed. Once the outer, woody leaves had been torn off and the beards scooped out, the delicate green hearts would be put in a solution of water and lemon to prevent them from discolouring. Papà would be in charge of thinly slicing them to create his much-loved spring salad, while Mamma mixed them with eggs and pecorino for her exquisite artichoke gratin. Any leftovers would be blanched, then pan-fried in peppery extra virgin olive oil and garlic. Heaven!

Coffee break with
Mamma and Papá at
our family home in Torricella.

INSALATA *di* CARCIOFI *e* PECORINO

◆ RAW ARTICHOKE AND SHAVED PECORINO SALAD ◆

Strolling around the local markets in Italy is a true feast for the eyes. In spring, the stalls proudly display the most beautiful artichokes a passionate home cook could dream of – from spiky dark-green ones and round, thornless ones right down to the stunning purple variety. When the produce is so blessed it is best to prepare it simply in order to fully appreciate its unique flavour. This salad is Papá's favourite way to pay his respects. And, quite frankly, it's the only thing he can cook!

SERVES 4–6

2 lemons
6 artichokes
2–3 tablespoons extra virgin
   olive oil
salt flakes
200 g pecorino, thinly shaved
10–12 mint leaves

1 Squeeze half of one lemon into a large bowl filled with water, then throw the squeezed lemon into the bowl, reserving the other half to rub onto the cut surfaces of the artichoke as you clean them.

2 Cut the top off an artichoke (about one third of the head) with a large serrated knife and remove all the thorns. Rub lemon over the cut edge. Next, cut off the stem using the same knife. (We don't need the stems for this recipe, but you can use the trimmed stems for a risotto or to throw them into your next minestrone.)

3 Beginning at the bottom of the choke, start to pull off the darker, outer leaves. Continue to do this until you are left with the pale-green heart. Clean up the edge of the chokes with a paring knife. Cut the heart in half and rub the cut sides with lemon, then scoop out the beard with a teaspoon or paring knife. Thinly slice the heart, then plunge the slices into the acidulated water until you are ready to use them. Repeat with the remaining artichokes.

4 To assemble the salad, drain the artichoke slices and season with olive oil and salt. Arrange on a serving plate and top with the shaved pecorino, mint leaves and a squeeze of juice from the remaining lemon.

◆ *Shaved parmesan makes a great alternative to pecorino.*

TORTINO di CARCIOFI GRATINATO

• ARTICHOKE GRATIN •

Italian home cooks are masters when it comes to not wasting food. Stale bread in particular is given a new lease of life in all kinds of ways. Here it is soaked in milk and added to eggs and sharp pecorino cheese. This batter envelops juicy artichoke hearts and is baked to golden perfection, resulting in a gorgeous vegetarian supper.

SERVES 6

6 artichokes
1 lemon, cut in half
2–3 tablespoons fresh
   breadcrumbs (see page 27)
150 g stale bread, crusts
   removed
4 tablespoons milk
6–7 oregano leaves,
   plus extra to garnish
2–3 tablespoons flat-leaf
   parsley leaves
7 eggs
200 g pecorino, grated
salt flakes and freshly ground
   black pepper

1 Prepare the artichokes as in the previous recipe (see page 99) and plunge into acidulated water (using one lemon half) to stop them going brown.

2 Preheat your oven to 200°C (180°C fan-forced). Oil a 24 cm tin or ovenproof dish and dust the base and sides with breadcrumbs.

3 Bring a large saucepan of salted water to the boil. Drop in the remaining lemon half and the cleaned artichokes and boil over medium heat for 4–5 minutes or until soft. Drain and set aside.

4 Meanwhile, place the bread, milk and herbs in a food processor and pulse 6–7 times or until a paste is formed. Set aside.

5 Crack the eggs into a large bowl and beat with a fork. Add the pecorino and the bread paste and whisk well. Season with salt and pepper, then pour half the mixture into the prepared tin or dish. Drain the artichoke halves and arrange them over the batter in a circle, then pour the remaining batter over the top. Scatter over the remaining breadcrumbs and bake for 25–30 minutes or until the gratin is nicely puffed up and has turned an irresistible bronze colour. Garnish with extra oregano leaves and serve.

♦ *This dish is equally tasty served warm or at room temperature, and will keep in the fridge for up to 2 days.*
♦ *You can use marinated artichokes if you don't have time to clean and blanch them yourself.*

CARCIOFI *in* PADELLA
• SAUTÉED ARTICHOKES •

rtichokes are so cherished at the Italian table we have devised endless ways to devour them: steamed, deep-fried, stuffed, sautéed and even raw. Whichever way suits you, know that each and every green layer is a miraculous health bomb. The spiny flower bud is high in fibre and antioxidants, and is particularly adept at aiding digestion and cleansing the liver – which makes it an essential friend when nursing a hangover. Trust me, I swear by it!

SERVES 4

1 lemon, cut in half
4 artichokes
2 tablespoons extra virgin
    olive oil
150 ml white wine
salt flakes and freshly ground
    white pepper
flat-leaf parsley leaves,
    to garnish
lemon juice, to serve

1   Squeeze the lemon into a large bowl filled with water and throw in the squeezed lemon halves. Clean the artichokes (see page 99), then cut the hearts in half and plunge them into the acidulated water.

2   Blanch the artichokes in salted boiling water for 10 minutes. Drain and set aside.

3   Heat the olive oil in a medium heavy-based frying pan over medium–high heat, add the artichoke hearts and sauté for 2–3 minutes. Pour in the wine and cook for 1–2 minutes or until the alcohol has evaporated. Turn off the heat, season with salt and pepper and serve warm or cold with a scattering of fresh parsley and a squeeze of lemon.

•   *If you can, drop a few lemon slices into the boiling water when blanching the artichokes to help preserve their bright-green colour.*

Abruzzo has a population of just over 1.3 million, making it one of the least populated regions in Italy.

FRITTATA *alle* ERBE *con* CAPRINO

• HERB FRITTATA WITH GOAT'S CURD •

Frittata, a rustic Italian-style omelette, has been a family favourite since time immemorial. Nonna Irene would never let us face a car trip longer than an hour without a stash of panini con frittata to make the journey sweeter, and Mamma would regularly make this simple, yet scrumptious meal to feed the family mid-week, or for a frugal Sunday supper. Admittedly, my frittata-making skills don't come close to hers – the lady who was proclaimed The Queen of Frittatas by my gluttonous husband. Mamma makes easy work of flipping the frittata without so much as a drop of egg spilling on the splashback. It is truly wonderful to behold. Alas, I resort to the more user-friendly way of sticking the pan under a hot grill to finish off the cooking process, but I do encourage you to have a go at this flipping caper. You never know, you may be named Queen or King of Frittatas in your own kingdom!

SERVES 4

8 eggs

3 tablespoons finely chopped chives

3 tablespoons roughly chopped flat-leaf parsley

a few marjoram leaves

4–5 mint leaves, roughly chopped

2 tablespoons milk

2 tablespoons freshly grated pecorino

salt flakes and freshly ground white pepper

4–5 tablespoons extra virgin olive oil

about 200 g goat's curd

1 Turn on the grill function in your oven.

2 Beat the eggs in a large bowl with a fork or whisk, then whisk through the herbs, milk and pecorino. Season with a little salt (keep in mind pecorino packs a sharp, savoury punch) and pepper and set aside.

3 Heat the olive oil in a medium non-stick, ovenproof frying pan. Drop in the egg mixture and swirl the pan around to distribute it evenly over the base. Using a wooden spoon or a spatula, move the egg around as it cooks to encourage the remaining liquid mixture to set. When the bottom looks almost cooked and the top is about to set, but is still a little wet, dollop the goat's curd on top.

4 Place the pan under the grill for 1–2 minutes to set the top of the frittata and colour the curd slightly.

5 Slide the frittata onto a serving plate and enjoy with greens, toasted bread or whatever takes your fancy.

• *The combination of herbs I suggest here is my absolute favourite, but really you can use whatever you have to hand.*
• *Any leftover frittata will make a nutritious filling for panini or school sandwiches.*

PIZZA RUSTICA
con BIETOLA

• SAVOURY TART WITH CHARD •

S avoury pies made with olive oil pastry feature often at the Italian table, accompanied by a green salad and a splash of wine. Nutrient-rich Swiss chard makes a perfect filling, married with sheep's ricotta and chunks of prosciutto, for a salty kick. Its sturdy leaves hold up better than spinach when cooking and its versatility ensures it can be used in soups as well, or simply sautéed with garlic and chilli for a side dish with attitude.

SERVES 6–8

2 cups (300 g) plain flour
75 ml extra virgin olive oil
3 tablespoons white wine
pinch of salt flakes
3–3½ tablespoons cold water
1 egg, mixed with
    2 tablespoons milk

CHARD FILLING
1 bunch Swiss chard or
    silverbeet, well washed
    and central rib removed
400 g fresh full-cream ricotta,
    well drained
4 eggs
½ cup (150 g) diced salami
    or soppressata (omit for
    a vegetarian version)
salt flakes and freshly ground
    black pepper
½ teaspoon freshly grated
    nutmeg
finely grated zest of ½ lemon

1   Place the flour, olive oil, wine, salt and 3 tablespoons water in a food processor and pulse 10–12 times or until the mixture resembles wet sand. Add the remaining water if the dough is too dry. Tip the dough onto a bench and gently press it together with your hands. Shape it into a flat disc, taking care not to overwork it or the pastry will be tough. Cover with plastic film and rest in the fridge for 30 minutes.

2   Preheat your oven to 200°C (180°C fan-forced). Grease and flour a 20 cm tart tin.

3   Take the dough out of the fridge and roll it out with a floured rolling pin to a thickness of 3–4 mm. Fold it into three, then roll it out to the same thickness again. Gently place it in the tart tin and trim the edges, reserving any scraps for later. Place the tin in the fridge while you make the filling.

4   To make the filling, blanch the chard or silverbeet leaves in salted boiling water for 2–3 minutes. Drain, then plunge them into ice-cold water to preserve their intense emerald hue. Drain again and set aside. Place the ricotta in a large bowl and beat until creamy. Add the eggs and salami or soppressata (if using) and season with salt, pepper and nutmeg. Stir in the lemon zest and cooked chard.

5   Pour the filling into the chilled tart shell. Decorate the top in a lattice pattern using the reserved pastry scraps, then brush with egg wash. Bake for 30–35 minutes. Remove and cool in the tin at room temperature before serving warm or cold.

FAGIOLI *e* RAPE

◆ BROCCOLI RABE AND BORLOTTI BEANS ◆

This is an ancient dish from Montesilvano, a charming medieval citadel on the Adriatic coast. It used to suffice as a main course accompanied by some cheese or a slice of frittata, but these days it is often served as a side dish or as part of an antipasto platter. It is a nutritious meal that will shatter the common misconception that Italian food is unhealthy and somewhat excessive. If you are using dried beans, they will need to soak overnight so start the recipe a day ahead.

SERVES 4

400 g shelled borlotti beans, or 1 cup (200 g) dried beans or 2 × 400 g tins borlotti beans, well drained
1–2 bay leaves
4–5 peppercorns
800 g broccoli rabe (see Note)
3 tablespoons extra virgin olive oil
2 cloves garlic, finely chopped
1 chilli, finely chopped (optional)
salt flakes

1 If you are using dried beans, soak them in water overnight, changing the water once or twice and discarding any that float to the surface. Drain, then place the soaked beans in a saucepan and cover with water. Add the bay leaves and peppercorns and simmer for 1½ hours or until tender. Leave in the saucepan until you are ready to use them.

2 If you are using freshly shelled borlotti beans, place them in a saucepan and cover with water, add the bay leaves and peppercorns and simmer for 30–35 minutes or until tender. Leave in the saucepan until you are ready to use them.

3 Tinned beans don't need any preparation other than draining.

4 Cook the broccoli rabe in a saucepan of salted boiling water for 1–2 minutes, then drain and plunge it in iced water to preserve its forest-green hue. Drain and roughly chop.

5 Heat the olive oil in a medium frying pan over medium–high heat and cook the garlic and chilli (if using) for 1 minute or until fragrant. Drain the beans, discarding the bay leaves and peppercorns but reserving 4–5 tablespoons of the cooking water. (If you are using tinned beans, just add some fresh water.) Add the beans and rabe to the pan, along with the reserved cooking water and stir-fry for 2–3 minutes or until all the flavours have mingled nicely. Taste for salt and adjust accordingly. Serve with slices of toast or frittata (see page 107) or white wine unleavened bread (see page 86).

◆ If broccoli rabe is hard to come by at your local market, replace it with broccolini.

PEPERONATA

• SWEET AND SOUR CAPSICUM •

Peperonata has always been on offer at our Sunday table. A perfect combination of sweet and sour capsicum and onion, stewed to perfection and coated gently in luscious extra virgin olive oil, just like my dear Great Aunt Italina used to make. Peperonata would definitely feature on the long list of food I would consume as my Last Supper. Indeed this was the case when Italina met her maker. The robust 94-year-young Abruzzese lady was found happily at rest in her bedroom, as a pot of sweet-smelling peperonata slowly bubbled away on her stovetop.

SERVES 4

3 tablespoons extra virgin
   olive oil
4 golden shallots, thinly sliced
2 cloves garlic, skin on,
   bashed with the back
   of a knife
5 capsicums (pepper)
   (red, yellow or green),
   seeds and membrane
   removed, cut into strips
3 tablespoons white
   balsamic vinegar
1–1½ tablespoons caster
   sugar, to taste
salt flakes
1 cup (260 g) tinned
   crushed tomatoes
basil leaves, to serve

1 Heat the olive oil in a large heavy-based frying pan over medium heat and cook the shallot and garlic for 2–3 minutes or until the shallot has softened and the garlic smells fragrant. Add the capsicum, vinegar, sugar and a pinch of salt and cook for 1–2 minutes, then pour in the crushed tomatoes. Reduce the heat to low, cover with a lid and leave to stew gently for 20–25 minutes.

2 Remove the lid and increase the heat to medium–high, then cook for 1–2 minutes to reduce the liquid further. Taste for salt and adjust accordingly. Turn off the heat, top with basil leaves and serve hot, warm or cold.

• *Zia Italina's peperonata makes a mean side dish for fried eggs.*

CALZONI con CACIOCAVALLO e PEPERONATA

• BREAD POCKETS WITH CHEESE AND STEWED CAPSICUM •

Typical of Abruzzo and Molise, caciocavallo (literally, cheese on horseback) earned its name from the way a mound of stretched cheese similar to mozzarella is rope-bound and dangled over a wooden board to age. It is generally mild in flavour, slightly salty with delicate grass and fruit aromas. This versatile cheese is always a welcome presence in an Italian pantry as it makes a lovely addition to a cheese and salami board, as well as a perfect filling for savoury pies or – my personal favourite – mini calzoni.

MAKES 8

1 quantity pizza dough
   (see page 132)
200 g caciocavallo, cut into
   small cubes
1 quantity peperonata
   (see page 112)
extra virgin olive oil,
   for drizzling
salt flakes

1 Preheat the oven to 220°C (200°C fan-forced). Line a large baking tray with baking paper.

2 Cut the dough into 8 pieces and roll out on a floured surface into discs about 3–4 mm thick. Arrange the cheese and peperonata over half of each disc (reserving any juices from the peperonata), then fold the other half over the filling. Pinch the edges to seal and shape the parcels into crescents.

3 Place the calzoni on the prepared tray, then brush with the reserved peperonata juices and drizzle a little olive oil over the top. Sprinkle with salt flakes and bake for 20–25 minutes or until nicely risen and beautifully golden. Serve hot, warm or at room temperature.

• Feel free to add spicy salami or soppressata to these parcels, if you feel in need of meat.

MACCHERONI alla CHITARRA con FIORI di ZUCCA e ZAFFERANO

• NOODLES WITH ZUCCHINI BLOSSOM AND SAFFRON SAUCE •

Maccheroni alla chitarra is an ancient type of pasta made by forcing a thinly rolled pasta sheet through a chitarra, a wooden frame strung with fine metal wire, similar to a guitar. The cut pasta is left to air-dry for up to 2 days to allow the surface to roughen up enough to retain the sauce, something your palate will be thankful for. However, I am hardly ever organised enough to roll my noodles with a few days to spare, and I promise you the result is just as rewarding if you let them sit at room temperature for 30 minutes. Traditionally maccheroni alla chitarra are tossed in rich meat sauces, with a preference for lamb, goat or the less mainstream rooster. It is no mystery that I have a certain weakness for a rich slow-cooked meat ragù, but occasionally, when I am after light, delicate flavours, I marry the thin strands with a touch of spring sweetness, rendered golden with a sprinkling of saffron threads.

SERVES 4

1 quantity of egg pasta dough made with 3 eggs and 2 cups (300 g) type '00' flour (see page 149), rolled into 3 mm thick sheets
semolina or polenta flour, for dusting
5–6 zucchini (courgettes), blossoms attached
4 tablespoons extra virgin olive oil, plus extra for drizzling (optional)
2 golden shallots, thinly sliced
2 cloves garlic, skin removed, bashed with the palm of your hand
4 tablespoons hot water infused with 1 teaspoon saffron threads
20 g butter
salt flakes and freshly ground white pepper
roughly chopped flat-leaf parsley, to serve

1 If you happen to have a chitarra frame, position the pasta sheet onto it, then use a rolling pin to press it down on the metal strings to obtain your noodles. Lift the noodles out, dust them with semolina and set aside. If you are using a pasta machine, pass the rolled sheets through the spaghetti setting, then dust the noodles with semolina.

2 Separate the zucchini from their blossoms. Cut the zucchini into small rounds and set aside. Gently open the yellow flowers and remove the stems, then cut the petals into 1 cm thick strips.

3 To make the sauce, heat the olive oil in a large heavy-based frying pan over medium heat, add the shallot and garlic and cook for 1–2 minutes or until fragrant. Add the zucchini rounds and cook, tossing regularly, for 4–5 minutes or until golden. Stir in the saffron-infused water and butter. Add the zucchini petal strips and remove from the heat – the residual heat will wilt them slightly. Taste for salt and adjust if needed.

4 Meanwhile, bring a large saucepan of salted water to the boil, add the pasta and cook for 2 minutes or until al dente. Drain, reserving a few tablespoons of the pasta cooking water. Toss the pasta in the sauce, adding some of the cooking water if necessary. Finish with a grinding of white pepper, a scattering of parsley and a drizzle of olive oil, if liked. Serve hot.

Making maccheroni
alla chitarra using my
great-grandmother's
instrument.

People - and dogs - strolling on
the jetty in Marina di San Vito

COUSIN MIRIAM'S RECIPES

◆ ◆ ◆ ◆ ◆ ◆ ◆

My maternal nonna's surname was Di Sangro, and given that her village is situated in the Di Sangro Valley, you can count on meeting distant relatives and second cousins once removed on every corner. This was the case recently when my mamma was reunited with a long-lost cousin from San Vito, a gorgeous seaside village on the Abruzzese coastline. In the traditional Italian way, once introductions had been made, family connections established and everyone had finished venting about recent political events, the ladies started talking serious stuff: food. It turns out cousin Miriam owns the best seafood restaurant in Marina di San Vito. I packed my bags immediately and travelled to meet her in the hope she'd share some of her extensive culinary knowledge with me. In the best Abruzzese spirit, she generously opened the door to her house and her kitchen. We spent a delightful afternoon reminiscing about family members, as we chopped, rolled, stewed and devoured the two heavenly seafood dishes that follow.

Marina di San Vito, Adriatic Coast.

Cousin Miriam let me have a go in her professional kitchen!

In good company with Miriam, Vincenzo and the cooking team at Lido Esperia, Marina di San Vito.

Early morning fishing
with Signor Sergio

Fossacesia, Abruzzo

TACCONCELLI
con RAGÙ di PESCE

• HOMEMADE PASTA SQUARES WITH FISH STEW •

This is a cross between a pasta dish and a seafood stew. It is traditionally served in individual terracotta pots, topped with a little chilli oil.

SERVES 4

4 tablespoons extra virgin
    olive oil
1 small brown onion, chopped
1 clove garlic, chopped
½ green capsicum (pepper),
    seeds and membrane
    removed, cut into
    small cubes
200 ml white wine
600 ml tomato passata
2 cups (500 ml) water
salt flakes
2 × 700 g barramundi
2 squid tubes, cleaned and
    cut into small strips
8 large scampi
chilli oil (see facing page), to
    serve (optional)

PASTA DOUGH
2 cups (300 g) type '00' flour
pinch of salt flakes
200–225 ml water, plus extra
    if needed
olive oil, for greasing
    your hands
semolina or polenta flour,
    for dusting

1 To make the pasta, put the flour and salt in a large mixing bowl, make a well in the centre, then slowly pour in the water, mixing as you go with a chopstick or your finger. Don't add all the water at once as you may not need it all. I would suggest you start with 200 ml and add the rest if needed. As a rule of thumb, a dry dough is easier to correct than a tacky one. Mix until the dough resembles wet crumbs, then tip it onto a floured surface, oil your hands and knead it for 3–4 minutes or until it comes together in a smooth ball. Cover it in plastic film and let it rest in the fridge for 30 minutes. You can make the dough a day ahead if you like.

2 Using a rolling pin or a pasta machine, roll out the dough to a thickness of 3 mm, then cut it into 2 cm squares. Dust them with flour so they won't stick together and lay onto a large platter or board dusted with semolina or polenta flour.

3 Heat the olive oil in a large saucepan over low–medium heat and cook the onion and garlic for 3–4 minutes. Add the capsicum and wine, then increase the heat to high and cook for 2–3 minutes or until the alcohol has evaporated. Add the passata, water and a pinch of salt and bring to a simmer.

4 Reduce the heat to low, add the barramundi and cook for 15–20 minutes or until cooked through. Lift out the fish, then extract the flesh and set aside. Meanwhile, drop the squid and scampi into the pan and cook for 2–3 minutes. Lift them out and set aside with the barramundi flesh.

5 Turn up the heat under the sauce, adding 1 cup (250 ml) water if it has reduced too much (you are going to cook the pasta in the liquid so there needs to be enough to cover it). When the sauce comes to the boil, drop in the pasta squares and cook for 1–2 minutes or until al dente. Add the seafood and mix through, then serve with a drizzle of chilli oil, if you like a bit of spice.

• *Chilli oil*
  To make your own chilli oil, roughly chop about 150 g dried chillies
  (available at Indian food stores, or dry your own if you have the
  patience) and place in a large sterilised jar. Pour in about 1 litre extra
  virgin olive oil (or enough to fill the jar), then seal the jar and store
  in a cool, dark place for at least 3 weeks before using. The heat and
  intensity of flavour will increase over time.

• *Miriam loves to use whole*
  monkfish, but as it is not readily
  available in Australia I have
  replaced it with barramundi.

COZZE RIPIENE *con* CHITARRINA

• HOMEMADE SPAGHETTI WITH STUFFED MUSSELS •

Maccheroni alla chitarra (see page 117) marry particularly well with seafood and turn this rustic dish into a truly special meal. Naturally you can replace them with fresh tagliolini (see page 244) or angel hair pasta.

~~~~~~~~~~~~~~~~~~~~~~~~~~~~~~~~ SERVES 4–6 ~~~~~~~~~~~~~~~~~~~~~~~~~~~~~~~~

150 g stale bread, crust removed, soaked in a little water until moist
2½ cups (200 g) grated pecorino
2 eggs
1 clove garlic, finely chopped
2–3 tablespoons finely chopped flat-leaf parsley, plus extra to serve (optional)
salt flakes
24 fresh mussels, cleaned and debearded
extra virgin olive oil, to serve

PASTA DOUGH
2⅔ cups (400 g) type '00' flour, plus extra for dusting
4 eggs
pinch of salt flakes

TOMATO SAUCE
3 tablespoons extra virgin olive oil
1 clove garlic, crushed
½ green capsicum (pepper), seeds and membrane removed, cut into large strips
800 ml tomato passata
pinch of salt flakes

1   To make the pasta dough, place the flour on a wooden board, make a well in the centre and drop in the eggs and salt. Mix together using your fingers or a fork, then knead vigorously for about 10 minutes. At first it will look crumbly, but once your body heat activates the starch in the flour the dough will change its texture, transforming into a smooth, firm ball. (If you want to speed things up you can mix the dough ingredients in a food processor until they resemble wet sand, then tip onto a floured board, bring together with your hands and knead for 1 minute.) Wrap the dough in plastic film and let it rest in the fridge for 30 minutes.

2   Meanwhile, to make the tomato sauce, heat the olive oil in a large heavy-based frying pan over medium heat, add the garlic and cook for 1 minute or until it starts to turn golden. Add the capsicum, passata and salt and simmer over low heat for 25–30 minutes, stirring occasionally.

3   Cut the dough into quarters. Work with one piece at a time and keep the rest wrapped in plastic film to prevent it from drying out. Flatten the piece of dough with the palm of your hand, then pass it through the pasta machine's widest setting three or four times, folding the dough into three each time. Continue passing the dough, each time through a thinner setting, until you get to the second-last setting or the sheet is roughly 2.5 mm thick. If you don't have a pasta machine, you can use a rolling pin and a lot of elbow grease.

4   Assuming you don't have a chitarra to hand (see page 117), pass the pasta sheets through the spaghetti/tagliolini cutter of your pasta machine. Liberally dust the spaghetti with flour to stop it sticking together and leave it to dry while you prepare the mussels.

5 Squeeze the water out of the bread and combine with the pecorino, eggs, garlic, parsley and salt. Set aside. Gently open the mussels using a knife, so that the valves are still attached but there is enough of an opening for the bread mixture to go in. Stuff each mussel with 1 teaspoon of the mixture, then close the valves, pressing with your fingers.

6 Put the mussels in the tomato sauce and cook, covered, over low heat for 10–15 minutes. The filling will puff up inside the shells and soak up all the beautiful tomato and garlic nectar as the mussels cook gently.

7 Shortly before the mussels are ready, bring a large saucepan of salted water to the boil, drop in the spaghetti and cook for 1–2 minutes or until al dente. Drain, reserving 4–5 tablespoons of the cooking water.

8 Dress the pasta with the tomato sauce, adding a little of the cooking water if you think the sauce needs it. Crown with the stuffed mussels, a little extra chopped parsley (if using) and a drizzle of extra virgin olive oil.

Stuffed mussels and their
sauce bubbling away.

With cousin Miriam at the back of her restaurant, Lido Esperia.

PIZZA con FRUTTI di MARE

• SEAFOOD PIZZA •

In the seaside villages of the Adriatic pizzas are often topped with freshly caught shellfish, a celebration of the riches of that coastline to crown everybody's favourite meal.

My top tip on pizza making is to give the dough time to prove slowly – in the fridge for at least 24 hours. It is this slow rising that will provide that essential light and crispy crust and perfectly risen cornicione (rim). Not to mention making it easy to digest. Even the most vehement I-don't-eat-wheat person will have to reconsider. I can proudly state that my recipe for pizza dough has won accolades from a few Paleo diet enthusiasts too. Mission accomplished! *Pictured page 134.*

SERVES 4

10 clams, rinsed well and kept
  in the fridge in a bowl of
  cold salted water
6 uncooked tiger prawns,
  peeled and deveined
  (see Note)
10 fresh mussels, cleaned
  and debearded
flat-leaf parsley leaves,
  to garnish

PIZZA DOUGH
2 teaspoons dried yeast
210 ml lukewarm water
1 teaspoon sugar
2⅔ cups (400 g) plain, type
  '00' or baker's flour
4 tablespoons spelt or
  wholemeal flour
2 teaspoons salt flakes
coarse semolina, for dusting
  (optional)

1 Start the pizza dough at least a day ahead. Combine the yeast, water and sugar in a bowl until frothy. Stand for 5 minutes. Put the flours in a large mixing bowl, pour in the yeast liquid and knead until combined, then add the salt. Turn out onto a floured cooking bench and knead vigorously for up to 10 minutes or until the dough is smooth, shiny and elastic. Add a little water if the dough feels too dry, but keep in mind that the more you knead it, the softer it becomes.

2 Alternatively, put the flours in the bowl of a stand mixer fitted with a dough hook, pour in the yeast liquid and let the machine work the dough on speed 1 for the first 2 minutes. Increase to speed 2 for 3–5 minutes, then work for 30 seconds on the highest setting. Tip the dough onto a floured surface, cover with a tea towel and rest for 30 minutes.

3 Stretch the dough with floured hands into a rectangle, then fold into three and shape into a ball. Place in an oiled container fitted with a lid. Make sure you use a large container that will allow room for rising. Rest the container in the fridge overnight (or for up to 3 days), to slow-prove and develop flavour and texture.

4 A couple of hours before you want to use the dough, remove it from the fridge and take off the lid. Cover loosely with a tea towel and leave at room temperature for 2 hours.

5 Meanwhile, prepare your tomato base (this can also be made the day before and kept in the fridge until ready to use). Heat the olive oil in a medium saucepan over medium–high heat, add the garlic, parsley stalks and chilli flakes (if using) and

TOMATO BASE

2 tablespoons extra virgin olive oil, plus extra for drizzling

3 cloves garlic, peeled and thinly sliced

1–2 tablespoons flat-leaf parsley stalks, finely chopped

1 teaspoon chilli flakes (optional)

150 ml white wine

400 g tin chopped or crushed tomatoes

salt flakes

◆ *Don't discard the prawn heads and tails. They will keep in the freezer for up to 6 weeks and, with the addition of olive oil, white wine, carrot and celery, can be turned into a magnificent fish reduction.*

cook for 1 minute or until the garlic is lightly golden and smells fragrant. Pour in the wine and cook over medium–high heat for 1–2 minutes or until the alcohol has evaporated. Add the tomatoes and a pinch of salt and simmer for 20 minutes. Turn off the heat and set aside until ready to use.

6 Preheat your oven to 220°C (200°C fan-forced). If you are using a pizza stone, put it in the oven now. For this recipe I like to use a large rectangular stone, but you could also use two small ones. Naturally, round baking stones are fine too.

7 Roll out the dough to a thickness of about 4 mm, using either a floured rolling pin or your hands. If baking on a stone, put the dough on a sheet of baking paper. Otherwise put the dough on a large baking tray lined with baking paper (you may need to use two trays, depending on the size of your oven). Spread the tomato base onto the dough and drizzle an extra 1–2 tablespoons extra virgin olive oil all over the pizza.

8 If using a baking stone, sprinkle the stone with semolina, then put the pizza (still on its baking paper lining) on the hot stone. Bake for 15 minutes. Meanwhile, rinse the clams again and drain them well. Gently open the door, peel the paper off the pizza base and add the seafood. Bake for a further 5–8 minutes or until the base is golden and slightly scorched, the shells have opened and the prawns are just cooked through. Serve immediately with a sprinkling of parsley leaves and a drizzle of extra virgin olive oil, if liked.

9 If you are using a baking tray, put the tray in the hot oven and bake for 15 minutes. Add the seafood and bake as above.

SEAFOOD PIZZA (see page 132)

Ceramic jugs at Lido Esperia.

The Adriatic coastline that runs between
Francavilla al Mare and Vasto is punctuated
by odd-looking fishing machines called
trabocchi. They look like bizarre wooden
insects, with long, swaying antennae reaching
for the water. In the old days they served as
ingenious fishing installations battling with
the fierce sea along the coast of Abruzzo, but
these days most of the trabocchi have been
converted into charming seafood restaurants.
Many tourists barely notice them, but for
those in the know, a trip to a trabocco
for lunch or dinner is an exquisite
culinary adventure.

'MPEPATA di COZZE

• MUSSELS IN PEPPER BROTH •

The reason Italians hardly ever order takeaway is that we have a vast repertoire of simple recipes that can be made in half the time you spend ordering your food and waiting for it to be delivered. And you can guarantee it will be much healthier and more exciting. This mussel recipe takes less than 10 minutes to cook. Add another 30 seconds for slicing the bread you will want to dip into the luscious broth, and 'tutti a tavola': everybody to the table!

SERVES 6

2 kg fresh mussels, cleaned and debearded
4 tablespoons extra virgin olive oil
2–3 cloves garlic, finely chopped
3 tablespoons finely chopped flat-leaf parsley stalks (only use the tender bit closer to the leaves)
200 ml white wine
salt flakes and freshly ground white pepper
flat-leaf parsley leaves, to garnish
crusty bread, to serve

1 Place the cleaned mussels in a bowl. Discard any that are already open or have a broken shell.

2 Heat the olive oil in a large heavy-based frying pan over medium heat. Add the garlic and parsley stalks and cook for 1–2 minutes or until fragrant. Pour in the wine and cook over high heat for 1–2 minutes or until most of the alcohol has evaporated. Add plenty of pepper, then drop in the mussels, cover with a lid and leave to steam. As the mussels open, lift them out with a slotted spoon and set them aside in a large bowl. Discard any that refuse to open. Taste for salt and adjust according to your taste. I often feel no need for extra salt as the liquid released by the mussels as they cook is pure sea-water nectar.

3 Pour the cooking liquid over the mussels and scatter with parsley leaves. Serve hot, with lots of crusty bread to dunk into that precious liquid.

• *These days you can buy vacuum-packed mussels, scrubbed clean and ready to go. They are available in two varieties: cooked and uncooked. Make sure you buy the uncooked ones.*

DITALINI RISOTTATI con VONGOLE e CECI

• DITALINI WITH CLAMS AND CHICKPEAS, COOKED RISOTTO-STYLE •

My older brother Giammarco is a chef and, along with passing on to me his fervour for Metallica and heavy-metal bands, he has also shared many tips and tricks of his cheffing trade. My most cherished new discovery is that you don't have to boil your pasta in a large pot of water: treat the noodles like risotto grains and let them absorb the sauce slowly and gently. Don't be alarmed by this change of method – this dish isn't at all labourious, especially if you stir with one hand and sip chilled Trebbiano with the other, all the while head-banging along to Master of Puppets. (OK, that last bit is optional!)

SERVES 4

4 tablespoons extra virgin olive oil

2 cloves garlic, 1 whole, skin removed and bashed with the back of your hand, 1 finely chopped

2 tablespoons finely chopped flat-leaf parsley stalks (use the tender middle bit, closer to the leaves)

1 small chilli, finely chopped (optional)

150 ml white wine

1 kg clams

350 g ditalini pasta

salt flakes

400 g tin chickpeas, drained and rinsed

2 tablespoons roughly chopped flat-leaf parsley

1 Fill your kettle with water and turn it on to boil.

2 Heat the olive oil in a large heavy-based frying pan (with a lid) over low–medium heat, add both cloves of garlic, the parsley stalks and chilli (if using) and cook for 1 minute or until the garlic starts to turn golden. Pour in the wine, then increase the heat to medium–high and cook for 1–2 minutes or until the alcohol has evaporated. Add the clams, cover with the lid and steam for 2–4 minutes to open the shells. As soon as they open, remove them with a slotted spoon to avoid overcooking them. (Discard any that do not open.)

3 Add the pasta to the pan, season it with a pinch of salt and then pour in enough water from the kettle to cover it. Boil the pasta for 3–4 minutes, then add the chickpeas and more water so the pasta is fully covered and cook, stirring regularly, for a further 3–4 minutes or until perfectly al dente.

4 While the pasta is cooking, take half the clams out of their shells. Discard the empty shells.

5 When the pasta is cooked, turn off the heat and return the clams and any juices they have released to the pan. Taste for salt and adjust accordingly, then top with a scattering of parsley and serve hot.

PASTA ROTTA con LENTICCHIE

• BROKEN PASTA AND LENTIL SOUP •

Mamma would often turn to this simple yet flavoursome soup to efficiently feed her three growing children. The lentils are stewed in homemade stock with onions, carrots, thyme, a chunk of pancetta and some pecorino rind for a rich, savoury punch. To finish, she would throw in broken bits of leftover dried pasta to thicken the soup and make it more substantial. Nonno Domenico used to alternate between a spoonful of soup and a bite of hot chilli, something I wasn't keen to try as a child, but have since become addicted to. Sometimes your legacy can chase you until you surrender to it!

SERVES 4

3 tablespoons extra virgin olive oil, plus extra for drizzling
3 golden shallots or 1 medium onion, roughly chopped
1 celery stick, thinly sliced
1 carrot, chopped
2 cm thick slice of pancetta or speck, cut into cubes
1 cup (220 g) puy lentils, rinsed under cold water
1 piece pecorino or parmigiano rind
1–2 sprigs thyme, plus extra leaves to garnish
3 cups (750 ml) vegetable or chicken stock, plus extra if needed
salt flakes and freshly ground black pepper
¾ cup (170 g) broken pasta (or use a small pasta such as ditalini or risoni)
2–3 cups (500–750 ml) boiling water
hot chillies, to serve (optional)

1 Heat the olive oil in a medium heavy-based saucepan over medium heat and cook the shallot or onion, celery and carrot for 3–4 minutes or until softened but not coloured.

2 Stir in the pancetta or speck and cook for 2–3 minutes over medium heat, then add the lentils, cheese rind, thyme, stock and a pinch of salt and simmer over low–medium heat for 25–30 minutes or until the lentils are almost cooked through.

3 Add the pasta and enough boiling water to cover the pasta and lentils and cook for 5–6 minutes or until the pasta is al dente and the lentils are cooked through. You will notice that the natural starch in the pasta acts as a thickener – add a little more water or stock if you prefer a more liquid soup. Remove the cheese rind, then season to taste with salt and pepper.

4 Ladle the soup into bowls and finish with a scattering of thyme leaves and a drizzle of olive oil. Serve with hot chillies if you fancy the Nonno Domenico experience!

• *You can make the lentil soup to the end of step 2 the day before you need it. The next day add 1 cup (250 ml) water and a pinch of salt, then bring it to the boil and cook the baby pasta as instructed in the recipe.*

SCRIPPELLE 'MBUSSE

• CREPES IN BROTH •

These delicate egg crepes are sprinkled with sharp pecorino cheese, rolled up and served with hot broth ladled over the top to create a rich and nourishing soup. Originally from Teramo, this dish has been a family Sunday supper for as long as I can remember. It shows how resourceful the Italian home cook can be. Even on the bleakest of days, when the pantry was bare, the fridge was empty and a trip to the shops was out of the question, Mamma could always combine a few essential ingredients and feed the appetite and the soul of her family. This dish comes with a distinctive sound memory: that of us unapologetically slurping the hot broth flavoured with the peppery bite of pecorino. If you can, start making the broth the day before. *Pictured page 146.*

SERVES 4

1¼ cups (100 g) freshly grated pecorino or parmigiano

BROTH
6 chicken wings
500 g mixed soup meat mix (such as short ribs, shanks, oxtail, bones and marrow)
1 onion, studded with 3–4 cloves
1 celery stick, cut into 3 pieces
1 carrot, cut into 3 pieces
2 tablespoons extra virgin olive oil
salt flakes
2 bay leaves

CREPES
3 eggs
400 ml milk
pinch of salt flakes
1⅔ cups (250 g) plain or type '00' flour
2 tablespoons melted butter
20 g butter, extra

1 To make the broth, preheat your oven to 220°C (200°C fan-forced). If you are using organic chicken wings, it is likely they will still have some plumage attached. To get rid of it simply flame them on your stovetop for 2–3 minutes or until the small feathers are burnt off.

2 Combine the chicken wings, meat mix, vegetables, olive oil and a pinch of salt in a large roasting tin and toss to combine. Roast for 30–40 minutes or until browned. Transfer everything to a large stockpot and cover with enough cold water to fill the pot by three-quarters. Add the bay leaves and 2–3 teaspoons salt and slowly bring to a simmer. Cook gently over low–medium heat for a minimum of 3 hours, skimming off the foam that comes to the surface during the first hour of cooking. Cooking it for longer will improve and concentrate the richness of the flavour. This is why you only season it with a little salt to start with, as the salt will concentrate too as the stock cooks.

3 After the stock has had enough time (up to 4–5 hours for a very meaty flavour), taste it again for salt and adjust accordingly. Remove the pot from the heat and let the broth cool at room temperature, then rest it in the fridge for at least 6 hours, preferably overnight. The fat will rise to the surface and create a lid to protect the broth underneath. Scrape the fat off with a spoon and discard it (preferably not down the drain as it may block your pipes). Strain the broth through a sieve to remove the solids.

Torricella Peligna

- *It is important to cook your broth slowly and gently. Cooking it over very high heat will cause the broth to become cloudy, as will over-stirring.*

4 You can more than halve the cooking time if you happen to have a pressure cooker. The other obvious advantage of this clever cooking gadget is that none of the precious aromas will escape as they are safely enclosed in a sealed environment.

5 To make the crepes, beat together the eggs, milk and a pinch of salt in a large mixing bowl. Gradually whisk in the flour to create a runny batter. Add the melted butter, then rest in the fridge for 30 minutes.

6 Melt the extra butter in a non-stick frying pan (or a crepe pan) over medium heat, ladle in a small amount of batter and tilt the pan so the base is covered in a thin layer of batter. Cook for 1–2 minutes or until the sides of the crepe start to lift off the pan and small bubbles form. Flip the crepe over and cook for 1 minute. Remove to a plate and repeat with the remaining batter. You want to make about 12 crepes altogether.

7 To serve, dust each crepe with a little bit of grated cheese, then roll them up to form cigars and place two or three in each bowl. Dust with plenty of grated cheese, then ladle the hot broth over the top. Garnish with any remaining pecorino, serve piping hot and get slurping.

CREPES IN BROTH (see page 144)

PASTA AND BEAN SOUP (see page 148)

SAGNE e FASCIUL'

• PASTA AND BEAN SOUP •

When Mamma and her sister Rita were young, Nonna Irene used to run a very successful dress-making business in Torricella. Indeed her creations were sought after from people near and far. Of course this meant that Mamma and my auntie didn't really see much of her – to this day, they can barely recall a family meal where everybody came together around an abundant table. Meals happened fast as the one table in the house doubled as Nonna's dress-making station, and the one room in the house served as a laboratory/bedroom/living room/dining room – you name it. Quite often Nonna would enlist the help of relatives to make sure her family was properly fed and looked after while she earned a crust (Nonno Domenico wasn't much chop at that working caper). Bisnonna Domenica, her mother-in-law, would happily come to the rescue. She was a lovely woman, with a good heart and lots of stories for the kids, but no cooking skills as such. One memorable day she decided to make sagne e fasciul' for the family . . . Everything would have been fine had she just stuck to the recipe, which called for lard. Alas, the inexperienced home cook picked up the white, lard-resembling bar of soap sitting by the kitchen bench and cooked up a cauldron full of soapy soup, bubbling away for all the wrong reasons!

My cousin Rosanna, who serves this soup as the signature dish in her restaurant Capè, gave me a very reliable recipe to share with you. As you will see I have replaced the lard with oil . . . just to be on the safe side! *Pictured page 147.*

SERVES 4

Cousin Rosanna and me at work

2½ cups (500 g) dried
   borlotti beans
1 potato, peeled
2 bay leaves
1 chunk of pancetta or speck
2 cloves garlic, peeled
salt flakes
3 tablespoons extra virgin
   olive oil
1 celery stick, thinly sliced
1–2 sprigs rosemary
1 small piece parmigiano
   or pecorino rind
2 × 400 g tins crushed
   tomatoes
2 cups (500 ml) chicken
   or vegetable stock
chilli oil (see page 127)
   or freshly ground
   black pepper
freshly grated parmesan,
   to serve

PASTA DOUGH
2 cups (300 g) type '00' flour
3 eggs
pinch of salt flakes
semolina flour, for dusting

◦ *Don't be tempted to use tinned
beans for this dish. Give it a bit
of love – you won't regret it.*

1 Soak the dried borlotti beans in water overnight, changing
the water once or twice. Drain.

2 Place the beans, potato, bay leaves, pancetta and 1 clove garlic
in a large saucepan of water, bring to a simmer and cook for
1–1½ hours or until the beans are tender. Season with salt.

3 While the beans are stewing away, make the pasta dough.
Place the flour on a wooden board, make a well in the centre
and drop in the eggs and salt. Mix together using your fingers
or a fork, then knead vigorously for about 10 minutes. At first
it will look crumbly, but once your body heat activates the starch
in the flour the dough will change its texture, transforming
into a smooth, firm ball. (If you want to speed things up
you can mix the dough ingredients in a food processor until
they resemble wet sand, then tip onto a floured board, bring
together with your hands and knead for 1 minute.) Wrap the
dough in plastic film and let it rest in the fridge for 30 minutes.

4 Cut the dough into quarters. Work with one piece at a time
and keep the rest wrapped in plastic film to prevent it from
drying out. Flatten the piece of dough with the palm of your
hand, then pass it through the pasta machine's widest setting
three or four times, folding the dough into three each time.
Continue passing the dough, each time through a thinner
setting, until you get to the second-last setting or the sheet
is roughly 2.5 mm thick. If you don't have a pasta machine,
you can use a rolling pin and a lot of elbow grease.

5 Pass the pasta sheets through the tagliatelle cutter of your
pasta machine. Lay the tagliatelle on a board and cut them
into 3 cm lengths. Gently place the cut noodles on a floured
tea towel, dust with semolina flour and allow to dry slightly
at room temperature.

6 Now, back to the stew. Transfer the potato, garlic, one third
of the beans and a few tablespoons of the stewing liquid to
a food processor and blend until smooth. Return the puréed
mixture to the pan.

7 Heat the olive oil in a medium saucepan over medium heat,
add the celery and cook for 2 minutes. Stir in the rosemary and
remaining garlic clove and cook for 1 minute or until fragrant.
Add the cheese rind and crushed tomatoes and simmer over
low–medium heat for 20 minutes or until reduced slightly.
Season with salt.

8 Add the tomato sauce to the bean mixture, then add the
stock and more salt if needed. Bring to the boil. Drop the pasta
straight into the soup and boil for 1–2 minutes or until cooked.
The starch in the pasta will make the soup deliciously thick.

9 Serve piping hot, finished with a drizzle of chilli oil or
a grinding of pepper and a handful of grated parmesan.

LE VIRTÙ
◆ CEREAL SOUP ◆

According to ancient pagan rites, every year on 1 May seven virgins were to each take seven ingredients to the city square, at which point those 49 ingredients were combined to create a soup. The soup marries winter and spring, and encourages the cleaning out of cupboards to welcome the impending bounty of the new season. My version only features 20 or so ingredients, but then again, I don't have the luxury of seven virgins gathering in my kitchen with their loot, so I make do with what's in my cupboard. The dried pulses need to be soaked overnight, so start this recipe a day ahead.

SERVES 6

½ cup (100 g) dried chickpeas
½ cup (100 g) dried borlotti beans
3 tablespoons dried kidney beans
3 tablespoons dried black-eyed beans
3 tablespoons extra virgin olive oil, plus extra to serve
1 onion, chopped
1 carrot, chopped
1 celery stick, chopped
1–2 sprigs thyme
100 g smoked pancetta or speck, cut into small cubes
1 piece pecorino or parmigiano rind
1 cup (200 g) barley
1 cup (200 g) farro
½ cup (110 g) puy lentils
3 tablespoons red lentils
3 tablespoons split peas
2 bay leaves
400 g tin tomatoes
1 medium potato, diced
salt flakes and freshly ground black pepper
½ cup (60 g) frozen peas
½ cup (60 g) shelled broad beans, skins removed

1 Soak the dried chickpeas and dried beans in water overnight, changing the water once or twice. Drain.

2 Heat the olive oil in a large saucepan over medium heat, add the onion, carrot, celery and thyme and cook for 2–3 minutes or until softened. Add the pancetta and cheese rind and cook for 1–2 minutes. Add the barley, farro, lentils, split peas, bay leaves and soaked chickpeas and beans, then pour in the tinned tomatoes and cover with enough water to two-thirds fill the pan. Bring to a simmer, then reduce the heat to low and cook gently for 1 hour.

3 Add the potato and cook for a further 1 hour, then taste to check that all the legumes are cooked through. Season well with salt. Add the peas and broad beans and cook for another 2–3 minutes or until just tender. Turn off the heat.

4 Ladle the soup into bowls and finish with a grinding of pepper and a drizzle of extra virgin olive oil.

◆ *Feel free to adjust the quantity and type of ingredients to suit your taste. Soaking a bag of mixed pulses overnight is a great idea and saves you measuring everything out. Pre-soaked porcini mushrooms also make a nice addition.*

AGRITURISMO TROILO

• • • • • •

One of my top tips for travellers venturing around Italy in search of authentic cuisine is to drive into the countryside, off the tourist path. Invariably you will find an unassuming sign pointing towards an agriturismo. Make this your stop! The principle behind an agriturismo can be summed up in just a few words: 'whatever we grow and breed will end up on your plate'! Such an alluring promise is enough to get my father driving 630 kilometres, from Milan to Colle Zingaro, to enjoy an unforgettable feast at Agriturismo Troilo. Antonina Troilo's cooking is simply sensational – you taste the stunning flavours as well as her pride and love for her legacy in every dish. There is nothing vain or showy about it – no pompous presentation, no elaborate food styling or abuse of micro herbs. It is just food at its honest, simplest best.

Buon appetito!

Talking food
(and drinking wine)
with Antonina

L'Agriturismo troilo

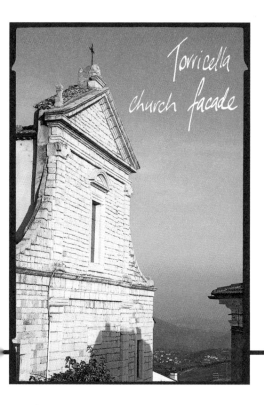

Torricella church facade

Torricella Peligna in the evening light

La Presuntuosa (the presumptuous) is a traditional charm given to young Abruzzese women when they come of age.

CANNELLONI di ANTONINA

• ANTONINA'S CANNELLONI WITH BRAISED MEAT •

Homemade pasta is a very popular main course at Italian family feasts. Forget about a roast with all the trimmings – we need our share of starchy goodness, made by hand with love. Naturally you can use store-bought dried cannelloni, but the flavour and texture won't be as luxurious. Especially if you follow Antonina's recipe of slow-braised meat enclosed in paper-thin sheets of fresh pasta, rolled into fat cigars and baked slowly, simply topped with a chunky tomato sauce.

〜〜〜〜〜〜〜〜〜〜〜〜〜〜〜〜〜〜〜〜〜〜 SERVES 6 〜〜〜〜〜〜〜〜〜〜〜〜〜〜〜〜〜〜〜〜〜〜

1 quantity of egg pasta dough
    made with 3 eggs and
    2 cups (300 g) type '00'
    flour (see page 149), rolled
    into 3 mm thick sheets

MEAT FILLING
3 tablespoons extra virgin
    olive oil
1 onion, finely chopped
600 g veal mince
salt flakes and freshly ground
    white pepper
350 g scamorza (see Note)
    or aged mozzarella,
    cut into cubes
3 eggs, lightly beaten
150 g freshly grated
    parmigiano

TOMATO SAUCE
3 tablespoons extra virgin
    olive oil
1 onion, finely chopped
1 carrot, finely chopped
1 celery stick, finely chopped
¼ red or green capsicum
    (pepper), in 1 piece
2 × 400 g tins tomatoes
    or 800 ml passata
salt flakes

1　To make the filling, heat the olive oil in a large frying pan over medium heat, add the onion and cook for 2–3 minutes or until softened. Add the mince and cook for 15–20 minutes, breaking up any lumps with a wooden spoon. Season with salt and pepper, then leave to cool for 10 minutes. Add the scamorza or mozzarella, egg and half the parmigiano, mix well and set aside to cool. You can make this up to a day ahead and rest it in the fridge, covered in plastic film.

2　To make the tomato sauce, heat the olive oil in a large frying pan over medium heat, add the onion, carrot, celery and capsicum and cook for 2–3 minutes or until softened. Add the tomatoes or passata and a pinch of salt and bring to a simmer. Reduce the heat to low and cook for 30 minutes, stirring occasionally.

3　Cut the pasta into 12 cm × 10 cm rectangles and blanch them in salted boiling water for 1 minute. Set aside to drain on clean tea towels without overlapping them. Place 2 tablespoons of the meat mixture in the middle of each rectangle and roll them up into cigar shapes to enclose the filling.

4　Preheat your oven to 200°C (180°C fan-forced) and grease a 45 cm × 30 cm baking dish.

5　Spread a ladleful of tomato sauce over the base and arrange all the cannelloni on top in a single layer, seam-side down. Cover with the remaining tomato sauce and sprinkle with the remaining parmigiano. Bake for 30–35 minutes or until golden.

〜〜

* *Scamorza is a cow's milk cheese similar to mozzarella, but with a more robust flavour. Enjoy it sliced, grilled or in toasted panini.*

ARROSTICINI

◆ MINI SHEEP SKEWERS ◆

Arrosticini are an Abruzzo speciality consisting of chunks of castrated sheep's meat, threaded onto skewers and barbecued over a specially crafted brazier until the fat is rendered and the meat forms an irresistible caramelised crust specked with salt flakes. In short, Abruzzo's own delightful sheep-meat kebabs. They are always a favourite at fairs and family gatherings, especially if accompanied by rustic chunks of bread and a glass or two of Montepulciano. They are pretty easy to make, but be warned: make sure you cook plenty. Once they hit the table, these delicious bites will disappear faster than you can imagine. Cook them over hot coals for the very best results.

MAKES 20–25

1 kg deboned sheep leg meat (use lamb if sheep meat is unavailable), cut into 1–1.5 cm cubes
salt flakes

1 Soak 20–25 bamboo skewers in water for 1–2 hours before adding the meat. This will stop them scorching during cooking.

2 Prepare your hot coals at least 30 minutes before cooking. Naturally you can grill the meat over a gas barbecue, but the flavour won't be quite as intense.

3 Thread the meat onto the skewers, making sure the fat layers are evenly distributed. You should aim to get 10–12 cubes of meat on each skewer. Grill the skewers over a moderate fire to prevent them from drying out, turning them regularly. They will take 15–20 minutes to cook through. Season with salt and serve piping hot.

◆ *You can prepare the skewers the day before and keep them in the fridge wrapped in butcher's paper or baking paper until you are ready to cook them.*

Snow-capped mountains of Abruzzo.

Signor Luigi of Terricella
Peligna, 94 years young.

AGNELLO CACIO e OVO

◆ LAMB WITH EGG, LEMON AND CHEESE SAUCE ◆

Traditionally, agnello cacio e ovo is eaten at the end of Lent to herald the Easter celebrations. It makes perfect culinary sense as this is the time of year when young lambs are ready for slaughter, although these days you may find 'Lamb cacio e ovo' served throughout the year in Abruzzese agriturismi. In my family we like to stick to tradition and enjoy this ancient and beautiful dish in springtime, preferably accompanied by freshly foraged wild herbs and salad leaves. If you can, make your own breadcrumbs by blitzing stale crustless bread in a food processor for about 10 seconds.

SERVES 4

12 lamb chops
8 eggs
2 cups (140 g) coarse
    breadcrumbs, preferably
    homemade
1 cup (80 g) grated pecorino
salt flakes and freshly ground
    black pepper
4 tablespoons extra virgin
    olive oil
3 cloves garlic, skin on,
    bashed with the back
    of a knife
2–3 sprigs thyme
juice of 1 lemon
lemon wedges, to serve

1 Pound the chops with a meat mallet to give an even thickness. Beat two eggs in a bowl and put the breadcrumbs in a large tray. Dip the chops in the egg first, then in the breadcrumbs to coat evenly. Set aside.

2 Beat the remaining eggs in a large bowl, then add the grated pecorino and a pinch of salt and pepper to taste, keeping in mind that pecorino is quite salty and sharp in flavour.

3 Heat the olive oil in a large heavy-based frying pan over medium heat. Add the garlic and thyme, then the chops, and pan-fry for about 2 minutes each side until golden brown. Remove the garlic cloves and thyme if you like, although I like the rustic look so I tend to leave them in.

4 Turn off the heat. Pour in the egg and cheese mixture and stir it through the chops (the residual heat will cook the eggs). Pour in the lemon juice and mix it through to arrest the cooking of the eggs (or they will start to curdle). Serve hot with lemon wedges. And a glass of Trebbiano!

◆ *I would highly recommend eating this dish as soon as it hits the table. Leftovers will keep well, but the egg will curdle once reheated.*

AGNELLO *alla* GRIGLIA *con* ASPARAGI

• GRILLED LAMB CHOPS WITH ASPARAGUS •

One undeniable truth about Abruzzese cooking is that its simplicity is deeply reliant on excellent produce. When you sit at the table of local trattorias or agriturismi, you are never presented with a menu, merely a waiter (generally the son or husband of the lady labouring in the kitchen), idly telling you what the core ingredient of that day's menu is. If you are in Abruzzo and they suggest agnello (lamb), nod enthusiastically. Forget about slow-roasted leg of lamb studded with garlic, rubbed in herbs and drizzled with a fancy jus. What you will be served are chops, grilled perfectly over coals, seasoned with plenty of salt. And maybe a single lemon wedge on the side. Maybe. Sometimes, however, you may come across a slightly more inventive cook and will find that your chops have been massaged with a heavenly garlic, rosemary and extra virgin olive oil paste. I usually have a preference for a simple squeeze of lemon over my grilled chops, but when I tried these divine savoury lollipops, I gobbled up everything on my plate and immediately wished for more.

SERVES 4

2 cloves garlic, peeled
   and left whole
2–3 sprigs rosemary
   (or try oregano)
salt flakes
2 tablespoons extra virgin
   olive oil, plus extra
   for drizzling
2 tablespoons white wine
16 lamb chops
16 spears asparagus, trimmed
   if necessary
mint leaves, to garnish
lemon cheeks, to serve

1 Place the garlic and rosemary in a mortar, add a pinch of salt and pound with the pestle until the garlic breaks down into a paste. Add the olive oil and wine and mix well. Set aside.

2 Bash the chops with a meat mallet. This process will tenderise the meat as well as increase the surface area the marinade has access to. Massage the chops with the garlic marinade, making sure they are evenly coated. Place the chops in a non-reactive bowl or plastic container, cover with a lid or plastic film and marinate in the fridge for 30 minutes.

3 Blanch the asparagus in salted boiling water for 1–2 minutes or until tender, but still firm to the touch. Drain, then rinse under cold water to preserve the vivid green colour. Season to taste with salt, then finish with a drizzle of extra virgin olive oil.

4 Heat up a chargrill pan or a coal barbecue. Cook the chops on both sides over very high heat until scorched but still succulent. The cooking time depends on the thickness of the chops and of course your personal taste, but as a guide, for medium, cook on both sides for 2–3 minutes. Cover the chops loosely with foil and rest for 5 minutes before serving.

5 Arrange the chops and asparagus on a large serving platter and garnish with mint leaves. Squeeze a little lemon juice over the top and serve hot.

CELLI PIENI

• GRAPE JAM CRESCENTS •

The liturgical rite of Corpus Domini has always been solemnly observed in Torricella. To celebrate the body of Christ in the Eucharist, the corso (the main street) is decorated with an infiorata – a colourful stream of flowers and petals – and exquisitely crocheted white linen sheets hang from balconies to symbolise purity and chastity. First communions are traditionally held on this day and it is a firm local ritual that one should fast the night before to ensure the body is a worthy temple in which to welcome Christ. It all sounds utterly romantic, but Mamma seems to have mixed feelings about her own first communion day in Torricella . . . Following tradition, she had fasted all night. But on that very special morning some well-intending relatives arrived to the house bearing gifts for the lucky girl: freshly baked celli pieni. Food. Satan! Mamma, an over-excited (and very hungry!) girl of nine, could not resist one little mouthful, and catastrophe struck! A family meeting was instantly called. What could be done to makes amends for such disgraceful behaviour? Zia Richetta, considered by everybody to be as wise as Solomon, decreed they would have to confess the shameful sin to Don Francesco (the priest) and seek his advice. The prelate promptly pronounced Mamma guilty. She could still march to church with all the other kids, but she would be publicly denied the white holy cracker as a reminder to other potential sinners out there. The poor girl! No wonder she grew up with a soft spot for her father's communist beliefs!

The filling for celli pieni is traditionally made with a special type of grape jam made from Montepulciano d'Abruzzo grape must. Naturally, you can replace this unusual ingredient with regular grape jam or a dark berry jam, such as blackberry or black cherry. The addition of vin cotto (a by-product of grape must) will bring out the 'grape-yness' in any case. For best results, start this recipe a day ahead. *Pictured page 168.*

MAKES 40

A view of the church in Torricella Peligna

1¼ cups (400 g) grape jam or
a dark berry jam
100 g toasted ground almonds
(see Note)
40 g dark chocolate, grated
finely grated zest of 1 lemon
3 tablespoons vin cotto
1 teaspoon ground cinnamon
⅔ cup (50 g) fresh
breadcrumbs (see page 27)
or crushed biscuits

PASTRY DOUGH
3⅓ cups (500 g) plain flour,
plus extra if needed
4 tablespoons caster sugar,
plus extra for rolling
150 ml extra virgin olive oil
½ cup (125 ml) white wine
4 tablespoons water

• *You can buy toasted ground
almonds at most supermarkets.
To toast and grind them yourself,
toss them in a frying pan over
medium heat for 1–2 minutes or
until fragrant. Allow them to cool
slightly, then place them in a food
processor and blitz until ground.*

1 Place the jam, almonds and chocolate in a medium saucepan
over low–medium heat. Cook for 3–4 minutes, stirring
occasionally, until thickened slightly. Turn off the heat.
Add the lemon zest, vin cotto, cinnamon and breadcrumbs
or crushed biscuits and mix well. Cool completely at room
temperature, then rest in the fridge for at least 8 hours,
or up to 3 days.

2 To make the pastry dough, put the flour in a large mixing
bowl. Make a well in the centre and add the sugar, olive
oil, wine and water. Work with your hands to bring the
ingredients together to form a smooth, soft dough. It needs
to be softer than pasta dough. Keep in mind that flour is very
sensitive to the weather, and on hot days you may need to
use less than on colder, drier days. If the dough is too wet,
add extra flour. Wrap the dough in plastic film and rest in the
fridge for 30 minutes. The dough can be made up to 3 days
in advance and kept in the fridge.

3 Preheat your oven to 180°C (160°C fan-forced). Line two
baking trays with baking paper.

4 Roll out the dough to a thickness of 2–3 mm, folding it
onto itself once or twice, either using a rolling pin or a pasta
machine. Cut the dough into 12 cm × 6 cm strips. Dollop
a teaspoon of filling on one half of each strip, then fold the
other half over the top. Cut around it using a knife or pastry
cutter to make a crescent shape and pinch the dough together
to safely enclose the filling.

5 Scatter some extra caster sugar onto a plate. Roll the celli in
the sugar, then place them on the prepared baking tray. Bake
for 18–20 minutes or until pale golden. Transfer to a wire rack
and allow to cool completely. They will keep in an airtight
container for 3–4 days.

GRAPE JAM CRESCENTS (see page 166)

CHICKPEA AND HONEY PASTRIES (see page 170) ➤

CALCIONETTI

• CHICKPEA AND HONEY PASTRIES •

Nonna Irene was a practical and down-to-earth woman, both very useful qualities in post-war Torricella, with two little girls to raise and a dreamer of a husband in tow! She set up a dress-making business from her living room, which quickly turned into a successful venture and Nonna's reputation as the best sarta (dress-maker) in the province of Chieti was soon established.

The workload was such that she had to enlist the help of young apprentices – cheap labour, you might call it. The young women felt very privileged to be admitted into Irene's workshop and would duly work long hours to impress her. Wedding dresses were always in demand and no bride would walk down the aisle without an Irene Di Sangro creation. People would speculate for months, trying to imagine what wonderful design Irene and her girls would conjure up. To fan this growing state of anticipation the bridal gown had to be kept a secret, so Nonna and her apprentices used to work at night, safe from prying eyes. To keep the apprentices' hands warm in the cooler months, a brazier would burn under the table, close to where young Loredana (Mamma) would be hiding, secretly listening to the gossip and scary accounts of ghost sightings. It was quite an advantageous location as she could hear without been heard, observe without been seen. One particularly cold night, Loredana's watchful eyes noticed that one distracted apprentice, Nina, accidentally put the hem of the precious dress right on top of the burning coals. Nina realised in horror that she was staring at an unmistakable burn mark. Had anyone noticed? No, she thought, and she decided to keep it a secret and cut off the burnt bit to fix it. Unsurprisingly, the more she cut, the more she had to cut to make it even . . . When Nonna Irene realised what had happened, she immediately asked who was responsible for such a catastrophe. Without blinking, Nina declared 'Loredana! It was Loredana!'. It was only years later that Nina apologised to Mamma and confessed her sin to Nonna. The fact that she brought around a large platter of sweet calcionetti – deep-fried pastries filled with chickpeas, honey and grape must – undoubtedly encouraged the ladies to forgive her on the spot. *Pictured page 169.*

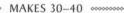

MAKES 30–40

San Giovanni in Venere Abbey

◆◦ ◆ ◦◆◦ ◆ ◦◆

1 quantity pastry dough
   (see page 167)
plain flour, for dusting
sunflower oil, for deep-frying
icing sugar, for dusting

FILLING
50 g blanched almonds
⅔ cup (70 g) walnuts
400 g tin chickpeas, drained
   and rinsed
150 g honey
3 tablespoons grape must
   or vin cotto
2 tablespoons chocolate chips
1 teaspoon ground cinnamon
1 tablespoon marsala or rum
   (optional)

1 Make the pastry, then wrap it in plastic film and rest at room temperature for 30 minutes to relax the gluten. Alternatively, refrigerate it for up to 3 days, and take it out of the fridge at least 1 hour before you intend to use it.

2 To make the filling, place the nuts in a food processor and blitz until they resemble coarse breadcrumbs. Remove. Add the chickpeas and blitz for 10–12 seconds or until creamy. Transfer the chickpea paste to a medium saucepan, add the honey, grape must or vin cotto, chocolate chips, cinnamon and marsala or rum (if using) and stir over medium heat for 2–3 minutes or until the chocolate has melted and the mixture is well combined. Add the nuts and mix well. Cool completely at room temperature, then rest in the fridge, preferably overnight, although 3–4 hours will do.

3 Dust your hands and working bench with flour to help you roll and shape the dough. Roll it out to a thickness of 2–3 mm, folding it onto itself once or twice, either using a rolling pin or a pasta machine, then cut it into 8 cm squares. Dollop a teaspoon of filling in the centre of each square and brush around the filling with water to moisten the dough. Fold one corner over to the opposite side to form a triangle and gently press around each mound to get rid of any air bubbles (otherwise the calcionetti may burst when you fry them). Cut around the sides with a pastry wheel to make them even, then lay the calcionetti on a platter lined with baking paper, taking care not to overlap them.

4 Half-fill a deep heavy-based frying pan with sunflower oil and heat over medium–high heat to 180°C or until a square of pastry sizzles straight away and browns in 15 seconds. Add the calcionetti in batches and cook for 2–3 minutes or until golden. Remove with a slotted spoon and drain on a plate lined with paper towel. Serve warm or at room temperature, dusted generously with icing sugar.

5 Calcionetti are best eaten within a few hours of being made but they will stay fragrant for 1 day, if you happen to have leftovers.

◦◦

◆ *If you would rather use dried chickpeas, soak 300 g dried chickpeas in water overnight, then drain and boil in fresh water for an hour or until tender. Proceed with the recipe.*

With my friend Adamo at Penna
Nera bar, Torricella Peligna

· DIALECT ·

Like all Italian regions, Abruzzo has its very own local dialect. Warm and colourful, with a sing-song tone, it bears just a faint resemblance to Italian as we know it. Depending on who is speaking, it can sound invitingly friendly or downright arcane. My late Great Uncle Eliseo and Great Aunt Italina spoke at such speed you'd quickly give up trying to comprehend and simply switch to nodding and smiling. My friend Adamo, on the other hand, makes an attempt to be intelligible and follows every sentence with a translation in Italian! His wit and humour never seem to suffer in the process.

Here are some examples of the Torricellano dialect and how it differs from Italian.

English: It's impossible to
change the mind of a fool
Italian: Hai voglia a fischiare se
l'asino non vuole bere
Abruzzese: Avoia a fiscà,
se l'asene ne vò vévere

English: It's impossible to please everyone
Italian: Chi la vuole cotta e chi la vuole cruda
Abruzzese: Chi le vo cott e chi le vo crude

English: He's good for nothing
Italian: Non sa neanche fare
la o co il bicchiere
Abruzzese: Ne nza fa mangh la
o che lu becchière

TARTELLETTE *allo* ZAFFERANO

• SAFFRON TARTLETS •

A little known fact about one of Italy's most famous dishes, risotto alla Milanese (saffron risotto Milan-style) is that the golden pistils used to colour and flavour the rice are likely to come from Abruzzo. The plains of Navelli are home to this precious spice, whose use is not uncommon in Abruzzese cuisine and can be traced back to medieval times. It suits sweet and savoury dishes alike and, as fond as I am of the Milanese signature dish, I find it even harder to resist these luxurious shortcrust tartlets filled with saffron-infused custard.

MAKES 16

100 g cold unsalted butter,
**   cut into cubes**
70 g almond meal
½ cup (80 g) icing sugar
1 egg
1⅓ cups (200 g) plain flour,
**   plus extra for dusting**

SAFFRON CUSTARD
2 cups (500 ml) milk
1 teaspoon saffron threads
4 egg yolks
90 g caster sugar
1 scant teaspoon cornflour

1 Place the butter, almond meal, icing sugar and egg in a food processor and process until combined. Add the flour and pulse four or five times until the dough resembles wet sand.

2 Tip the dough onto a bench and gently press it together with your hands. Shape it into a flat disc, taking care not to overwork it or the pastry will be tough. Cover with plastic film and rest in the fridge for 30 minutes.

3 Meanwhile, to make the saffron custard, heat the milk in a medium saucepan to just below simmering. Remove the pan from the heat, add the saffron and leave to infuse for 10 minutes – the milk will turn a golden yellow. In a medium bowl, beat the egg yolks and sugar until pale and fluffy. (You can do this by hand with a whisk or use hand-held electric beaters.) Add the cornflour and mix with a wooden spoon until combined.

4 Pour the milk into the egg mixture, whisking constantly until smooth and well incorporated. Pour the mixture back into the saucepan and bring to a gentle simmer, stirring constantly. Reduce the heat to low and cook, stirring, for 3–4 minutes or until it becomes thick and luscious. Pour the custard into a bowl and cover the surface with plastic film so it doesn't form a skin. If you are not using it straight away to fill the tart shells, allow the custard to cool at room temperature, then transfer to the fridge, where it will keep for up to 2 days.

5 Preheat your oven to 180°C (160°C fan-forced). Grease and flour 16 regular muffin holes.

• *If you have any unfilled pastry
cases left over, store them in
an airtight container at room
temperature. They will keep
well for 2–3 days.*

6 Take the dough out of the fridge and roll it out with a floured
rolling pin to a thickness of about 3 mm. Using a pastry cutter,
cut out circles to fit the muffin holes. Cut out circles of baking
paper to line the pastry cases, then fill each one with baking
beads or rice and blind-bake for 8–10 minutes. Remove the
baking paper and weights and return the pastry cases to the oven
for another 4–5 minutes or until pale golden and dry. Cool the
cases in the tin for 30 minutes, then gently take them out.

7 Fill the pastry cases with the custard and serve straight away.
Be sure to fill the cases just before serving to avoid soggy pastry.

BOCCONOTTI

• FILLED SHORT PASTRIES •

Typical of central Italy, these delicate pastries are filled with the holy trinity of patisserie: chocolate, cinnamon and toasted almonds. In Abruzzo this perfect filling is sometimes enhanced with dark berry jam and a drop of the local liqueur, centerbe, which is ideal for those who love intense aromas with a bit of a bang.

MAKES 12

150 g raspberry or
    blackberry jam
100 g ground toasted almonds
½ cup (95 g) dark chocolate
    chips
1 teaspoon ground cinnamon
1 tablespoon centerbe liqueur
    (optional; see Note)
icing sugar, for dusting

PASTRY
1⅓ cups (200 g) plain flour
½ teaspoon baking powder
90 g icing sugar, sifted
75 ml extra virgin olive oil
2 egg yolks
small pinch of salt flakes

1 Place the jam, almonds and chocolate in a small saucepan over low heat and stir gently for 2–3 minutes or until the chocolate has melted. Add the cinnamon and liqueur (if using) and set aside to cool. The filling can be stored in an airtight container in the fridge for 3–4 days.

2 To make the pastry, place the flour, baking powder and icing sugar in a large bowl. Pour in the olive oil, then add the egg yolks and salt and knead gently for 1–2 minutes or until it comes together in a smooth ball. If it is too dry add a few drops of water. Try not to overwork the dough otherwise the pastry will be tough. Cover with plastic film and rest for 30 minutes. If it is very hot, rest the dough in the fridge.

3 Preheat your oven to 200°C (180°C fan-forced).

4 Grease and flour 12 regular muffin holes. Cut the dough in half. Roll out one portion of dough to a thickness of 3 mm and lay it over the muffin tin, then gently press the pastry into the holes, leaving a little overhanging the sides. Roll out the remaining piece of dough and cut out 12 discs about one third larger than the muffin holes. Dollop 1 tablespoon of filling into each hole and cover snugly with a pastry disc, then cut away any excess dough. Gently press the edges to neaten and seal in the filling.

5 Bake for 18–20 minutes or until pale golden. Cool in the tin for a few minutes, then transfer to a wire rack to cool completely. Dust generously with icing sugar and serve.

◆ *Centerbe is an emerald-green Abruzzese liqueur, made from a variety of herbs and spices. It is incredibly high in alcohol and its zesty punch is rather an acquired taste. Unfortunately, despite being half Abruzzese myself, I don't think I have yet acquired it . . .*

PAN DELL'ORSO

◆ BEAR'S CAKE ◆

Pan dell'orso (bear's cake) bears its name (pun intended!) because according to legend, an Abruzzese shepherd guarding his sheep saved himself and his herd from a hungry Marsican bear by throwing a sack of these delicious treats right at the animal's snout. Unsurprisingly, the ferocious carnivore abandoned his primordial instinct to indulge in this almond and honey cake, lusciously coated in dark chocolate.

SERVES 8

6 eggs, separated
3 tablespoons honey
170 g caster sugar
60 g softened butter
1⅓ cups (160 g) almond meal
140 g self-raising flour, sifted
40 g spelt flour, sifted
2½ tablespoons milk
finely grated zest of 1 lemon
pinch of salt flakes

CHOCOLATE GLAZE
30 g unsalted butter
75 g dark chocolate chips
2 tablespoons glucose syrup
1 teaspoon vanilla paste
   or the seeds scraped from
   ½ vanilla bean
pinch of salt flakes
150 ml double cream
3 tablespoons brown sugar

1 Preheat your oven to 180°C (160°C fan-forced). Grease and flour a pudding basin.

2 Beat the egg yolks with the honey, sugar and butter until pale and creamy. Add the almond meal, flours, milk and lemon zest and mix to combine. Beat the egg whites with a pinch of salt until soft peaks form, then gently fold the whites into the batter.

3 Pour the batter into the prepared pudding basin and bake for 45–50 minutes or until a skewer inserted in the middle comes out clean. Remove and leave to cool in the basin for 1 hour, then turn out onto a wire rack to cool completely.

4 To make the chocolate glaze, put the butter, chocolate chips, glucose syrup, vanilla and salt in a small saucepan and stir over low heat until the butter and chocolate have almost melted. Add the cream and sugar and simmer gently, stirring occasionally, for 3–4 minutes or until the sugar has dissolved. Remove from the heat and cool for 5 minutes.

5 Place a sheet of baking paper underneath the wire rack. Slowly pour the chocolate glaze over the cooled cake, to cover evenly. Allow to dry and set before transferring to a platter and serving in slices.

◆ *Pan dell'orso is the less famous cousin of parrozzo, a dome-shaped cake made with maize flour typical of Pescara, a bustling seaside town in Abruzzo. The mountain version of this rich dessert replaces the yellow grain with rustic spelt and extravagant saffron with sticky honey. It is safe to assume both cakes are equally delightful!*

◆ *Traditionally ground bitter almonds are added to the batter. I have replaced them with plain almond meal as bitter almonds can be hard to come by.*

FIADONE di VINCENZO

• VINCENZO'S FIADONE CAKE •

People of Abruzzo seldom indulge in lavish cakes and pastries. When an occasion calls for a special dessert, though, the skilled and resourceful Abruzzese home cooks rely on an ancient and indulgent recipe for what is, effectively, an Italian cheesecake made with fresh ricotta, plenty of eggs and lemon. In the best tradition of regional home cooking, recipes are passed on and never altered, to honour the legacy they come with. Sadly for me, I didn't inherit a secret family recipe for this special cheesecake, but I have managed to acquire one from a most reliable source: the Di Cino family in Torricella. Their fiadone has won many prestigious awards and when the family patriarch Vincenzo departed, his legacy passed on to his children, so that they would continue to brighten the festive gatherings of Torricellani with this sweet offering.

SERVES 10–12

7 eggs
120 g caster sugar
finely grated zest of 1 lemon
300 g fresh full-cream ricotta
    (preferably homemade,
    see page 223)
300 g grated primo sale
    (see page 218) or paneer
2 tablespoons sambuca
    (optional)

DOUGH
1⅓ cups (200 g) plain or
    type '00' flour
1 egg
2½ tablespoons extra virgin
    olive oil
1½ tablespoons caster sugar
100 ml water

1   To make the dough, put the flour in a large bowl and make a well in the centre. Add the egg, olive oil, sugar and one third of the water and mix with a wooden spoon or your hands until a soft dough forms. If it is too dry and stiff, gradually add the remaining water until the desired consistency is achieved. Wrap the dough in plastic film and set aside to rest.

2   Beat the eggs, sugar and lemon zest for 3–4 minutes or until pale and fluffy. Add the ricotta, grated cheese and sambuca (if using) and mix until well combined.

3   Preheat your oven to 200°C (180°C fan-forced). Grease and flour a 24 cm ciambella tin (or other round tin with a hole in the middle).

4   Cut off a quarter of the dough and reserve. Roll out the rest of the dough to a thickness of 3–4 mm and use to line the base of the prepared tin, leaving some overhanging. Pour in the filling, then fold the overhanging pastry over the filling. Roll out the reserved dough to the same thickness and cut it into 3 cm squares. Dot them over the top as a finishing touch.

5   Bake for 45–55 minutes or until the pastry is golden and the filling is cooked through but still has a slight wobble in the middle. Remove from the tin immediately (so the pastry doesn't sweat) and cool completely. Fiadone will keep for up to 3 days, stored in an airtight container or wrapped in foil.

•   *The sambuca helps neutralise the dominant egg flavour in the filling. You can replace it with rum or amaretto, or lemon juice, if preferred.*

PIZZA DOLCE

◆ CELEBRATION SPONGE CAKE ◆

Pizza dolce is a sumptuous, alchermes-flavoured sponge cake typical of Abruzzo, layered with thick coffee-flavoured custard and topped with whipped cream and candied cherries. No family feast would be complete without it. No matter how full the bellies are after a day devoted to remorseless gluttony, we always find a bit of room to accommodate a morsel of pizza dolce. Best followed by a long, long pisolino (snooze) . . .

Start this recipe a day ahead, if possible, to give the sponge cake time to cool completely before you slice it.

SERVES 10

alchermes liqueur or coffee,
  for brushing the cake
1 cup (250 ml)
  whipping cream
2 tablespoons icing sugar
glacé cherries, to decorate

SPONGE CAKE
5 eggs, separated
150 g icing sugar, sifted
1 teaspoon vanilla paste
1 cup (150 g) plain flour
2 tablespoons potato starch
1 teaspoon baking powder
¼ teaspoon cream of tartar

CUSTARD FILLING
850 ml milk
1 vanilla bean, split in half
  and seeds scraped
rind of 1 lemon, in strips
6 egg yolks
½ cup (110 g) caster sugar
60 g cornflour
1 tablespoon cocoa powder,
  dissolved in 2 tablespoons
  hot coffee

1 Preheat your oven to 180°C (160°C fan-forced). Line a 25 cm square cake tin with baking paper.

2 To make the sponge cake, beat the egg yolks with the icing sugar and vanilla for 2–3 minutes or until pale and fluffy. Sift in the flour, potato starch and baking powder and mix gently to incorporate. Set aside. Beat the egg whites and cream of tartar in a clean bowl until soft peaks form. Gently fold half the egg whites into the batter to loosen it, then fold in the rest until the batter is smooth.

3 Pour the batter into the prepared tin and smooth the top using a spatula. Bake for 35–40 minutes or until golden and a skewer inserted into the middle of the cake comes out clean. Remove from the oven and cool in the tin for 20 minutes, then invert the cake onto a wire rack to cool completely.

4 Meanwhile, to make the custard filling, heat the milk in a medium saucepan to just below simmering. Remove from the heat, add the vanilla and lemon rind and allow to infuse for 10 minutes. In a medium bowl, beat the egg yolks and sugar until pale and fluffy. You can do this by hand using a whisk or with a hand-held electric beater. Add the cornflour and mix with a wooden spoon until combined.

5 Strain the infused milk, then gently pour it into the egg yolk mixture, whisking constantly until smooth and well incorporated. Pour the mixture back into the saucepan and bring to a gentle simmer, stirring constantly. Reduce the heat to low and cook, stirring constantly, for 3–4 minutes or until it becomes thick and luscious.

• *Potato starch is often used in Italian confectionery as it gives cakes and pastries an ineffable lightness. These days you can find it at most supermarkets or at Italian delis under the name of 'fecola di patate'.*

6 Spoon the custard evenly into two bowls. While it is still hot, add the cocoa and coffee mixture to one bowl and mix well to incorporate. Cover the custards closely with plastic film so they don't form a skin. Leave to cool at room temperature, then place in the fridge for at least 2 hours to firm up.

7 To assemble, cut the cake horizontally into three equal squares and brush with the alchermes or coffee. Place one square on a cake stand and spread with the chocolate and coffee custard. Cover this with a second square and spread with the vanilla custard. Top with the final layer of sponge.

8 Whip the cream and icing sugar until soft peaks form. Spread the cream over the cake and decorate with glacé cherries. Take to the table for you and your guests to enjoy.

CICERCHIATA

• HONEY-DRIZZLED CLUSTER CAKE •

Cicerchiata, also known as struffoli, takes its name from cicerchie, a small chickpea-like legume that is about the same size as the pellets of fried dough in this indulgent dessert. The little nuggets are shaped in a wreath and stuck together with copious amounts of honey. There is nothing grand or elaborate about it, yet it is quite impossible to resist.

As kids, we used to gallop to the table as soon as Nonna set a platter of cicerchiata on it. No matter how full we were after a festive meal, the miniature balls would inevitably disappear, leaving sticky finger prints all over the tablecloth. I have a sentimental attachment to this recipe. It is as if my nonna's presence is conjured up in my kitchen as soon as I start to fry the nuggets. It was certainly the case the day this photo was taken and I found my eyes filling with tears at the sight of my photography team nonchalantly picking at the dessert. Nonna would have smiled her unassuming smile as if to say, 'Really, you like it? Good for you!'

My nonna's recipe doesn't call for any embellishment to this glistening cluster of spheres, but there are many versions that see cicerchiata dotted with slivered almonds, lemon zest or coloured sprinkles. Over to you, really.

SERVES 6–8

3⅓ cups (500 g) plain flour
40 g butter, melted
40 g caster sugar
4 eggs
finely grated zest of 1 lemon
pinch of salt flakes
1 tablespoon grappa
   or sambuca
1–2 tablespoons water
   (optional)
light-scented olive oil or
   canola oil, for deep-frying
1½ cups (540 g) honey

1 Place the flour, butter, sugar, eggs, lemon zest, salt and grappa or sambuca in a large bowl and mix well to form a dough that is similar in texture to a pasta dough. If it is too dry, add the water, 1 tablespoon at a time. Cover with plastic film and rest in the fridge for 30 minutes.

2 Remove the dough from the fridge and shape it into ropes about 1.5 cm thick. Cut each rope into 1.5 cm squares and roll them to resemble chickpeas.

3 Half-fill a medium heavy-based saucepan with olive or canola oil and heat over medium–high heat. Test it by dropping in a piece of dough: if it sizzles straight away and turns golden in 15 seconds, the oil is ready. Turn the flame down if you think your oil is too hot.

4 Add the balls in batches and cook for 2–3 minutes or until golden brown. Remove with a slotted spoon and drain on a tray lined with paper towel.

5 When all of the balls are cooked, heat the honey in a medium saucepan until it thins to a pouring consistency. Add the fried balls to the honey and stir carefully until well coated. Remove from the heat and allow to cool for 5 minutes in the pan, stirring every so often.

• *You can make individual cakes using paper muffin cases. Wrapped in cellophane and tied with a pretty bow they make a lovely Christmas gift.*

6 Place an oiled glass or cup in the middle of a large serving platter, then mound the honeyed nuggets around the glass in the shape of a ring. Allow the honey to set and the cicerchiata to cluster nicely (about 3–4 hours), then remove the glass or cup to reveal the empty hole in the middle.

7 Serve as it is, or decorated with your choice of nuts, candied fruit or sprinkles.

Abruzzo is famous for the production of honey, saffron, pasta, red garlic, confetti (sugared almonds from Sulmona), sweet red capsicum from Altino, truffles, extra virgin olive oil and tobacco.

Antonina and me enjoying circerchiata and girls' secrets.

PESCHE al VINO con CREMA di MASCARPONE

• WINE-DRENCHED PEACHES WITH MASCARPONE CREAM •

Nonno Domenico would often wind up his summer lunches slicing a peach into the remnants of his wine. The golden, ripe fruit, bursting with sunshine and luscious juice, would absorb the last drops of Trebbiano like a sponge, under the eagle eyes of us kids. Those of us who had been particularly good would be allowed a taste of Nonno's concoction. Although I have turned this simple combination of flavours into an elegant dessert, its unpretentious spirit remains unaltered.

SERVES 4

4 white or yellow peaches
finely grated zest of 1 lemon
2–3 sprigs lemon thyme, plus
    extra leaves to garnish
400 ml white wine
2 eggs, separated
3 tablespoons caster sugar
250 g mascarpone
1 teaspoon vanilla paste
    or the seeds scraped
    from ½ vanilla bean
pinch of salt flakes
2–3 tablespoons flaked
    almonds

1 Cut the peaches into quarters and place them in a large bowl with the lemon zest and thyme. Pour in the wine and leave to macerate in the fridge for at least 30 minutes, and up to 2 hours.

2 Meanwhile, whisk together the egg yolks and 2 tablespoons sugar for 2–3 minutes or until pale and fluffy and the sugar has dissolved. Add the mascarpone and vanilla and mix through with a wooden spoon until light and creamy. Whip the egg whites with a pinch of salt until soft peaks form, then add the remaining sugar and beat until glossy. Gently fold into the mascarpone cream until combined. Cover with plastic film and rest in the fridge for at least 30 minutes.

3 Just before you are ready to serve, toast the almonds in a dry frying pan for 1–2 minutes or until golden and fragrant. Set aside in a bowl to cool.

4 Divide the peaches among four bowls and top with 1–2 tablespoons of the mascarpone cream. Drizzle over the macerating liquid, and crown with toasted almonds and a few extra thyme leaves.

• *You can make the mascarpone cream the day before, if you like. Cover it well with plastic film and store it in the fridge until needed.*

Majella Mountain, Abruzzo

Olive groves in Caprafico, Abruzzo

MOLISE

Molise is undoubtedly one of the lesser-known regions in Italy. Indeed, many Italians seem unsure of the whereabouts of this mysterious territory. I tried my luck throwing some questions out at a dinner party not long ago and while there were a few people who could name the two provinces and other snippets of trivia, just as many of my fellow diners responded with quizzical looks and vague comments indicating only faint familiarity with this region. Curious, isn't it?

I'm not quite sure why Molise doesn't enjoy a higher national and international profile, as it is a mine of artistic, historical and culinary riches, but maybe an elusive nature is not such a hindrance; it is because of its obscurity that one can experience that thrilling feeling of having stumbled upon an unchartered, exciting land, ripe for exploration.

This was certainly the case when I first travelled around Molise in my early twenties. I was touring Italy with theatre shows and very eager to absorb all the experiences I possibly could. I certainly made the most of the time I spent in one of the main provinces, Campobasso, exploring the vibrant old town and indulging in the excellent local produce and rustic cuisine. I sampled it all, from liver sausages to lamb offal ones (the famous torcinello, for hard-core meat lovers), from buffalo mozzarella still warm from its whey bath, right down to the most addictive chilli I have ever come across: diavolillo (the little devil). It was only because I was involved in a three-hour marathon on stage every night that I didn't end up two stone heavier!

The food wasn't the only thing that struck a chord with me. I was completely won over by the Molisani, with their affable, old-world manners and passionate temperament (think twice before getting into an argument on Italian politics around these parts!), but most importantly, their profound sense of regional pride. The Molisani will fight to protect their heritage and traditions. They gained their independence from Abruzzo with much fanfare in the early sixties, when the two regions, once united under the name of The Abruzzi, were separated. In the last 50 years the region has gradually established its own cultural and culinary identity, and although the kinship with neighbouring Abruzzo still exists, Molise proudly stands on its own, showcasing its unique personality, from the dialect spoken to the glorious local foodstuffs and the striking and unadorned beauty of the surroundings.

This spirit is perfectly represented in the local cuisine, the quintessential expression of Italian cucina povera (peasant cooking). Although the literal translation is 'poor cooking', there is nothing sparse or meagre about cucina povera – a cost-effective, rustic style of preparation that relies solely on seasonality and sustainability, brought together with one last fundamental ingredient: love. Molise is home to dishes such as slow-cooked goat ragù with hand-cut noodles (see page 252), stuffed capsicums enriched with piquant pecorino (see page 230) and an exquisite yet ferociously spicy octopus stew (see page 246). But just when you think you can confidently associate Molisana country cooking with bold, robust flavours, you will be offered a delicate platter of pink sponge cakes resembling blushing peaches, sandwiched together with luscious custard cream (see page 266).

My strongest advice when travelling around Molise is to visit the old stone-wall villages lodged between the valleys, such as Pietrabbondante, Civitanova del Sannio or Castellino del Biferno. Although most of the population has moved to the bigger cities, their natural beauty remains unaltered and somewhat adrift in time, making the trip a truly unique experience of a bygone Italy.

Molise really has it all: from the stunning ancient churches and ruins, to the wild paths used for transhumance, right down to the blue shores – each discrete landscape offering its own bounty, ready to unveil and fall in love with. ❧

Pietrabbondante, Molise

The coastal town of Termoli, Molise.

The region's most famous wines are stamped
with the coveted Di Origine Controllata
(DOC) mark. These are Biferno, Molise
and Pentro. I have a particular fondness
for Biferno rosé, a perfect blend of
Montepulciano, Trebbiano and Aglianico
grapes. It marries beautifully with slices
of grilled primo sale cheese (see page 218),
another specialty of Molise.

Sourdough bread proving

PIZZA
di SAN MARTINO
◆ SAINT MARTIN ROLLS ◆

Legend has it that on a cold and stormy November night, Martino, a Roman soldier, crossed paths with a naked beggar. The soldier generously cut his cloak in half to share its warmth with the less fortunate soul. As soon as Martino set off again on his journey the rain ceased and the temperature rose, heralding a brief but very welcome Indian summer – one that has recurred every autumn ever since. Every year on 11 November Italy celebrates this most peculiar weather phenomenon, known as Estate di San Martino (Saint Martin summer), with the merry consumption of food and vino novello (new-season wine). The Molisani like to bake a special cluster of rolls in the shape of a wreath, each containing a particular seed or dried pulse. Which roll you choose is not a decision to be taken lightly as each has its own traditional meaning. If you are the lucky recipient of a broad bean, you can rightfully call yourself 'The Queen of the House'; however, should your roll conceal a dried borlotti bean, you will be dubbed 'the cuckold'. The one you really don't wish to receive though is the chickpea, which signifies . . . ehm . . . 'the flatulent'!

<hr>

MAKES 8

<hr>

3 cups (450 g) self-raising flour
¾ cup (60 g) grated pecorino
3 tablespoons fennel seeds
2 teaspoons salt flakes
½ cup (125 ml) extra virgin olive oil
200 ml water, plus extra if needed
mixed dried pulses or seeds, such as broad beans, borlotti beans, chickpeas, sunflower seeds or pumpkin seeds
1 egg, mixed with 2 tablespoons milk

1 Preheat your oven to 200°C (180°C fan-forced) and line a baking tray with baking paper.

2 Combine the flour, pecorino, fennel seeds and salt in a large bowl, add the olive oil and water and mix with a wooden spoon until a dough forms. If it is too dry, add a little more water.

3 Tip the dough onto a floured surface and knead for about 3 minutes or until smooth. Divide the dough into eight balls. Flatten the top of each ball with your hands, place a seed or dried pulse in the middle, then roll it back into a ball. Arrange the balls close together on the prepared baking tray in the shape of a wreath. Brush the top with egg wash and bake for 25–30 minutes or until golden and cooked through.

4 Serve warm and observe your fellow diners as they discover their true selves!

<hr>

◆ *These rolls are best eaten on the day they are baked.*

PANINI ALL'OLIO

• OLIVE OIL BREAD CRESCENTS •

Italians would never dream of going on a picnic without a good supply of freshly baked panini, to stuff with a few simple ingredients or to simply dunk in piquant, emerald extra virgin olive oil. Having said that, I would suggest that very few Italians would actually go to the trouble of baking the rolls from scratch, seeing as the local bakeries sell them fresh and fragrant at a reasonable price. You know me, though – I leap with joy at any excuse to get stuck into some sort of dough, and I enthusiastically took on the challenge to come up with a delicious formula that produces a soft and irresistible panino, so flavoursome it can proudly stand on its own.

〜〜〜〜〜〜〜〜〜〜〜〜〜〜〜〜〜〜〜〜 MAKES 8 〜〜〜〜〜〜〜〜〜〜〜〜〜〜〜〜〜〜〜〜

2 teaspoons dried yeast

1 egg

2 tablespoons extra virgin olive oil, plus extra for oiling the bowl

100 ml water

2¾ cups (410 g) baker's flour, plus extra if needed

2 teaspoons salt flakes

1 egg, extra, lightly beaten

PRE-FERMENT (BIGA)

½ teaspoon dried yeast

2 cups (500 ml) lukewarm water

1 cup (160 g) durum wheat flour

3 cups (450 g) baker's flour, specialty bread flour or plain flour

1 To make the biga, dissolve the yeast in the water in a large bowl, add the flours and mix with a wooden spoon until you have a thick batter. Cover it with plastic film and rest in the fridge overnight or at room temperature for 2½–3 hours until bubbly and risen.

2 If you have rested the biga in the fridge overnight, take it out 1 hour before kneading so it returns to room temperature.

3 Add the yeast to the biga and mix it in with a wooden spoon until combined. Add the egg, olive oil, water and flour and combine with a wooden spoon. Tip the dough onto a floured surface and knead well for 5 minutes. If the dough feels too sticky, add a little more flour, keeping in mind that this is supposed to be a soft dough, but it should come away easily from your fingers.

4 Stretch the dough into a rectangle, add the salt and knead well for another 5 minutes or until shiny and smooth. Shape it into a ball, then place in a large oiled bowl. Cover with a damp tea towel and leave it to prove at room temperature for 1 hour.

5 Take the dough out of the bowl and knock it back to deflate it. Stretch it into a rectangle, fold it into three and then shape it back into a ball. Return the dough to the oiled bowl and leave it to prove at room temperature for 1½–2 hours or until it has doubled in size.

6 Place the dough on a floured surface and divide it into eight portions. Flatten each portion with your hands or a rolling pin, then roll it onto itself to shape a crescent. Place the crescents on a large baking tray lined with baking paper, dust with flour and leave to prove for 45–60 minutes. Leave plenty of room for spreading as they will increase in size.

• *Try not to be put off by the thought of making a ferment to build your dough. The flavour and texture of your bread will be vastly improved if you don't skip this essential step.*

7 Preheat your oven to 220°C (200°C fan-forced). Place an empty metal bowl in the base of the oven to heat up.

8 Just before baking, brush the tops with beaten egg, then carefully slide the tray into the oven. Fill the heated metal bowl with cold water to create steam, then spray the top of the crescents with water. Close the oven door and bake for 20–25 minutes or until golden and the bottom sounds hollow when tapped with your finger. Transfer to a wire rack to cool. Enjoy them just as they are or fill them with your favourite cold meat and cheese for the ultimate panino experience!

Church of San Bartolomeo, Campobasso

CROSTINI
con RICOTTA e SPINACI

• CROSTINI WITH LEMON RICOTTA AND SPINACH •

Although most Italians are famously fond of dunking cakes and pastries in coffee for breakfast, the peasant tradition of central Italy is often more about the consumption of sturdier meals that celebrate the simplicity of its regional produce. Stale bread is never wasted in those kitchens and comes to new, noble life when topped with piquant local olive oil and freshly made ricotta. Enjoy this for breakfast or lunch.

SERVES 4

3 cloves garlic

4 thin slices of day-old sourdough

2½ tablespoons extra virgin olive oil, plus extra for drizzling

200 g fresh full-cream ricotta (see page 223)

finely grated zest of 1 lemon

freshly ground white pepper

300 g baby or English spinach

¼ teaspoon freshly grated nutmeg

salt flakes

lemon juice, to taste

1 Preheat your oven to 220°C (200°C fan-forced). Line a baking tray with baking paper.

2 Cut one garlic clove in half and rub the bread slices with the cut sides. Brush both sides of the bread with some of the olive oil. Place the bread on the prepared tray and bake for 10 minutes each side or until golden and crisp. Set aside at room temperature.

3 Meanwhile, place the ricotta, lemon zest and pepper in a bowl and mix until smooth and creamy.

4 Bash the remaining garlic cloves with the back of a knife. Heat the remaining olive oil in a frying pan over medium–high heat, drop in the garlic and cook for 1–2 minutes or until fragrant. Add the spinach and cook, covered, for 2–3 minutes until wilted. Season with the nutmeg, a pinch of salt and a squeeze of lemon juice. Remove the garlic.

5 Arrange the crostini on a serving platter. Spoon over the lemon ricotta, arrange the spinach on top and drizzle with a little extra olive oil.

• *Nutmeg is never missing from any Italian pantry. We love to add it to meat sauces or vegetable dishes to enrich them with its warm, nutty aroma.*

PIZZA *di* FARRO *con* SOPPRESSATA *e* PATATE

◆ NO-KNEAD SPELT PIZZA WITH SOPPRESSATA AND POTATOES ◆

Soppressata is a cured pork-based salami that has been squashed slightly and is therefore 'pressato' (flat); the spicing varies from place to place according to local tradition, and in Molise tends to vary from family to family. Very much like salami, it is eaten just as it is with local fresh bread – often as a morning snack. The addition of soppressata to spelt pizza takes the concept of 'snack' to a higher level, possibly even that of a proper meal! Spelt is a highly nutritious ancient grain that seems to be enjoying a renaissance amongst home bakers with an interest in healthy eating. It contains a higher percentage of protein than white wheat and the flavour is nuttier and more robust.

SERVES 6

1⅓ cups (200 g) strong
    baker's flour
1⅓ cups (200 g) spelt flour
100 g wholemeal spelt flour
340 ml water
½ teaspoon dried yeast
pinch of sugar
salt flakes
1 medium potato, thinly sliced
2 tablespoons extra virgin
    olive oil
1–3 sprigs rosemary (optional)
150 g thinly sliced soppressata
    (hot or mild, according to
    your liking)

1 Mix the flours, water and yeast together with a wooden spoon until combined. Add the sugar and 1 teaspoon salt and mix well – your mixture will look and feel quite sticky and does not require kneading. Cover the bowl with plastic film and prove the dough at room temperature for 10–14 hours or until it is bubbly, wet and considerably grown in size. At this point, you can use the dough as your pizza base or you can rest the bowl in the fridge, well covered with plastic film, for up to 5 days. The flavour and structure of the dough will improve the longer you slow-prove it.

2 Preheat your oven to 220°C (200°C fan-forced). Line a baking tray with baking paper.

3 While the oven is heating, cook the sliced potato in a saucepan of salted boiling water for 5 minutes. Drain gently, season with salt and set aside.

4 Tip the dough onto the tray and spread it out with wet hands to the desired shape. Top with the softened potatoes, drizzle with the olive oil and add a little rosemary, if liked. Bake for 15 minutes, then add the soppressata and bake for a further 10–15 minutes or until the crust is caramel brown and the bottom is crisp. Serve warm or at room temperature.

◆ *When shaping the dough be mindful not to burst the air bubbles that have formed during the slow fermentation. These coveted air pockets hold the secret to a light-as-a-feather crust.*

HOMEMADE CHEESE

* * * * * * *

Before you think me mad, let me assure you that this kind of cheese making is easier than you may think. No peculiar ingredients, arcane kitchen tools or refined skills are required. Primo sale is the cheese made from cow or sheep's milk at its earliest stage of maturation. In simple terms, it is the first curds that separate from the whey, which are left to drain and set in a mould until firm enough to be sliced. It is milky white in colour and mild in flavour and can be enjoyed as it is or grilled, very much like haloumi. The obvious advantage of making primo sale from scratch is the marvellous 'siero' you are left with, the whey. This is the crucial ingredient needed to make ricotta, a most loved cheese in these parts. Ricotta is obtained by reheating the leftover whey with full-cream milk and a few drops of lemon juice to encourage more curds to form. Really, it is too easy not to have a go. I can predict that once you taste your very own freshly made ricotta, still warm from its mould and drizzled with honey or extra virgin olive oil, you will embark on a life-long love affair with this spectacular by-product of cheese making.

PRIMO SALE

• HOMEMADE PRIMO SALE CHEESE •

Cheese making comes easier if you can get your hands on cheesecloth or muslin and a perforated mould, either plastic or wooden. But if you don't have these things to hand, there is nothing an ingenious mind can't overcome: a white tea towel or even an old white t-shirt will work just as effectively, as will a colander and a fine-mesh sieve.

MAKES 250 G

2.5 litres full-fat cow's milk
250 g thick Greek yoghurt
2 tablespoons lemon juice
pinch of salt flakes

1 Put the milk and yoghurt in a medium non-reactive saucepan and stir to combine. Bring it to just below the boil, then add the lemon juice and salt and mix well for 1 minute. Remove the pan from the heat, cover with a lid and stand at room temperature for 15–20 minutes to allow the mixture to coagulate and separate into curds and whey.

2 Line a cheese mould or colander with a double layer of wet muslin, cheesecloth or a damp tea towel and set it over a large bowl. Strain the mixture through the mould or colander and press it to compact it well. You will be left with the hot curds, while the whey is collected in the bowl underneath. Leave to drain at room temperature for 10–15 minutes.

3 When it's cool enough to handle, gather the corners of the cloth into a bundle and try to squeeze out most of the whey. Place the bundle, still in the cloth, back in the mould or colander to drain further and set. I often put a weight on it to help extract the whey faster. Stand at room temperature for 30–60 minutes.

4 Remove the cloth. Return the set cheese to the mould for 1 hour, then turn it over to dry it further at room temperature for 10–12 hours or until set. Enjoy fresh or store in the fridge for up to a week.

• *Don't discard the whey you have collected! It is the essential ingredient needed for homemade ricotta (see page 223).*

PRIMO SALE *alla* PIASTRA *con* VERDURE

• GRILLED PRIMO SALE AND VEGETABLE SALAD •

I like to use a non-stick pan for this recipe, to avoid cooking with excess fats. You can use a regular pan if you prefer – just make sure you brush the vegetables and cheese with olive oil on both sides, to prevent them from sticking.

SERVES 4

3 zucchini (courgettes),
  thinly sliced lengthways
1 large eggplant (aubergine),
  thinly sliced
2–3 tablespoons extra virgin
  olive oil
salt flakes
500 g primo sale cheese
  (see page 218), left to
  mature for at least 2 days
  (up to 1 week)
basil and mint leaves,
  to garnish
juice of ½ lemon

1 Heat a non-stick chargrill pan or non-stick frying pan over high heat and cook the vegetables for 2–3 minutes on each side. Arrange them on a large platter and drizzle with olive oil. Season with salt.

2 Cut the cheese into 1 cm thick slices and grill on both sides for 1–2 minutes or until softened. Place the cheese on the vegetables and scatter over the herbs. Squeeze a little lemon juice over the top and serve as a light lunch.

• *If primo sale is hard to find or making it from scratch does not agree with your lifestyle, you can use paneer or haloumi instead.*

RICOTTA FATTA
in CASA

◆ HOMEMADE RICOTTA ◆

Having spent half of my childhood romping around the hills of central Italy, sampling exquisite dairy products, I can confidently call myself a ricotta connoisseur. I stand by the simple rule that life is too short to bother with the low-fat variety or anything watery that comes in a plastic tub. If you can't get yourself a large wedge of fresh ricotta from a reputable deli, you might as well make it yourself. This is how.

MAKES 250 G

1.5 litres full-fat milk
1 litre whey (see page 218)
2 tablespoons lemon juice
pinch of salt flakes

1 Rinse out a large saucepan (this will prevent the milk from scorching), then combine the milk and whey in the pan. Bring it to just below the boil, then add the lemon juice and salt and mix well for 3–4 seconds. Remove the pan from the heat, cover with a lid and stand at room temperature for 15–20 minutes to allow the mixture to coagulate and separate into curds and whey.

2 Line a ricotta mould or colander with a double layer of wet muslin, cheesecloth or a damp tea towel and set it over a large bowl. Ladle the liquid into the cloth and leave to drain for at least 30 minutes but no more than 2 hours. The longer you leave it to drain, the firmer it will become.

3 Remove the cheese from the cloth, then return it to the mould to emboss it with its wired pattern. Serve warm, spread on bread or toast or drizzled with honey, or place it in an airtight container with a ladleful of whey to keep it moist and store it in the fridge for up to 2 days.

◆ *The leftover whey can be frozen for up to 4 weeks and used to make fresh cheese or as a replacement for buttermilk.*

CROSTATA con RICOTTA, CIOCCOLATO e CILIEGE

• RICOTTA, CHOCOLATE AND CHERRY TART •

Who said that rustic food needs to be frugal? As much as I have a special fondness for homely cooking, I have to confess a certain weakness for anything pretty. This gorgeous tart is the best of both worlds: a short, nutty pastry that houses a chocolate surprise, a luscious ricotta filling spiked with orange liqueur, and a topping of succulent ruby cherries. Perfect!

SERVES 8–10

150 g dark chocolate chips
400 g fresh full-fat ricotta,
    well drained (see page 223)
200 ml thickened cream
4 tablespoons icing sugar
1 teaspoon vanilla paste or
    the seeds scraped from
    ½ vanilla bean
finely grated zest of 1 orange
1 tablespoon orange-scented
    liqueur
about 20 cherries, to garnish

ALMOND SHORT PASTRY
100 g cold unsalted butter,
    cut into cubes
70 g almond meal
½ cup (80 g) icing sugar
1 egg
1⅓ cups (200 g) plain flour,
    plus extra for dusting

1 To make the pastry, place the butter, almond meal, icing sugar and egg in a food processor and process until combined. Add the flour and pulse four or five times until the dough resembles fine, wet sand.

2 Take the dough out of the bowl. Gently press it together with your hands and shape into a ball, taking care not to overwork it or the pastry will be tough. Cover with plastic film and rest in the fridge for 30 minutes.

3 Preheat your oven to 180°C (160°C fan-forced). Grease and flour a 24 cm springform tin.

4 Take the pastry out of the fridge and roll it with a floured rolling pin between sheets of plastic film or baking paper to a thickness of 3 mm. Gently lift the pastry into the prepared tin to line the base and sides. Don't worry if it tears – just pat it back in place with your fingers. Try to work quickly so the dough doesn't warm up and soften too much.

5 Cut out a disc of baking paper and place it on top of the pastry. Cover it with baking beans or rice and blind-bake for 8–10 minutes or until pale golden. Remove the baking paper and weights and return the pastry case to the oven for another 10–15 minutes or until golden. Cool in the tin for 1 hour, then gently take it out. Allow to cool completely.

6 Melt the chocolate chips in a heatproof bowl set over a saucepan of barely simmering water, stirring occasionally (make sure the bowl doesn't touch the water). Remove from the heat. Using oven mitts, take the bowl of chocolate to your work bench and brush the pastry shell with enough molten chocolate to coat it. Allow the chocolate layer to cool, then store the tart shell in an airtight container for up to 2 days.

7 Beat the ricotta with the cream and icing sugar until smooth, then add the vanilla, orange zest and liqueur and mix well.

8 To assemble, simply spoon the filling into the pastry case, top with cherries and enjoy.

Jesus gives the hills of Molise his blessing!

Scamorza cheese, Agnone

I ROSE CH'À PASTELLA

◆ BATTERED CAULIFLOWER FLORETS ◆

Molise is a fiercely peasant region, its culture and identity so deeply intertwined with the rugged shape of its mountains and coastline. And yet the local vernacular has given the humble cavolfiore (cauliflower) a most romantic name: the rose. No matter how homely and unadorned this dish is, I cannot help but feel in the mood for romance as I prepare my firm white roses, ready to be turned into golden buds.

SERVES 4

1 kg cauliflower, broken into
    florets, then washed and
    well dried
olive oil, for deep-frying
2 eggs, lightly beaten
150 ml sparkling water
⅔ cup (100 g) self-raising flour
salt flakes and freshly ground
    white pepper

1 Bring a large saucepan of salted water to the boil. Drop in the cauliflower florets and cook for 5 minutes, then drain and allow to dry.

2 Half-fill a deep heavy-based frying pan with olive oil and heat over medium–high heat.

3 In the meantime, whisk the eggs and sparkling water into the flour and season with salt and pepper.

4 Test the oil by dropping in a teaspoon of batter: if it sizzles straight away and turns golden in 15 seconds, the oil is ready. Coat the florets in batter, shake off the excess then drop them into the oil in batches. (Don't overcrowd the pan otherwise the oil temperature will drop, resulting in rather soggy florets.) Cook for 3–4 minutes or until crisp and golden, then remove with a slotted spoon and drain on paper towel.

5 Season the florets with a little extra salt and serve hot as an antipasto or to accompany pre-dinner drinks.

◆ *Be sure to drain the florets well after boiling. The drier they are when dipped into the batter and fried, the crisper they will be.*

PEPERONI IMBOTTITI

• STUFFED CAPSICUM •

Most regions of Italy have a version of this dish. Whether they are made with mince meat or adapted for those who favour a vegetarian diet, they are all invariably delicious. In this version, sweet capsicums are stuffed with ricotta, breadcrumbs and hot chillies and baked until bursting with goodness. I am yet to find a meat lover who doesn't devour these wholesome parcels with the same gusto they would gnaw on a rib-eye steak!

MAKES 4

4 green or red capsicums (peppers)
400 g fresh full-fat ricotta (see page 223)
4 tablespoons fresh breadcrumbs (see page 27)
¾ cup (60 g) freshly grated pecorino
1 egg
4–5 basil leaves, roughly chopped
2–3 tablespoons finely chopped flat-leaf parsley
salt flakes and freshly ground black pepper
4 tablespoons extra virgin olive oil, plus extra for drizzling (optional)

1 Preheat your oven to 200°C (180°C fan-forced). Line a baking dish with baking paper.

2 Wash the capsicums, cut off the tops and scoop out the white membrane and seeds. Place the capsicums in the prepared baking dish.

3 Mix together the ricotta, breadcrumbs, pecorino, egg and herbs in a large bowl and season to taste with salt and pepper. Spoon the mixture into the capsicums until three-quarters full, then drizzle a tablespoon of olive oil over each one. Drizzle extra oil all over the capsicums if desired.

4 Bake for 30–35 minutes or until a golden crust has formed. Serve hot or at room temperature.

• *When buying ricotta, I tend to steer clear of the kind sold in tubs as it is often too watery. Get a nice, firm slice from your local deli, if possible, or make your own if you feel adventurous (see page 223).*

BROCCOLINI RIPASSATI

• BROCCOLINI COOKED WITH CHILLI AND GARLIC •

Over the last decade broccolini has begun to enjoy well-deserved acclaim. As soon as nutritionists unveiled its boundless health benefits and chefs and home cooks started sharing their favourite ways to consume it, we have all fallen in love with these elegant green stems. Even my children, who would rather skip a day at the beach than eat anything remotely green, find broccolini ripassati a palatable proposition. And it has nothing to do with me yelling at them in Italian and threatening to never allow them to watch cartoons again. Nothing at all.

SERVES 4

2 bunches broccolini
3 tablespoons extra virgin olive oil
2 cloves garlic, skin on, bashed with the back of a knife
1 diavolillo or bird's eye chilli, finely chopped
pinch of salt flakes

1 Blanch the broccolini in a large saucepan of salted boiling water for 5 minutes.

2 Meanwhile, heat the olive oil in a medium frying pan over low–medium heat, add the garlic and chilli and cook for 1–2 minutes or until softened.

3 Drain the broccolini straight into the frying pan, and toss over medium heat for 1–2 minutes or until the broccolini is nicely coated in the chilli and garlic oil. Season with salt and serve as a side dish or by itself with some cheese and bread.

• *Rabe (rapini) or broccoli florets make a worthy alternative, should broccolini be unavailable.*

INSALATA di LENTICCHIE e PEPERONI

• LENTIL AND CAPSICUM SALAD •

This glorious recipe is yet another example of just how healthy our regional peasant cuisine can be. Lentils are used abundantly in Italian recipes, both for their versatility and nutritional value. They are high in fibre and protein and are an excellent source of magnesium and folate. As so often happens with modern food trends, cafés, restaurants and health food stores seem to have discovered this powerful gift of nature, and they pop up in pretty much everything, from soups and salads to croquettes and even cookies. Move over quinoa – the lentil has its sights on your crown!

SERVES 4

1¼ cups (275 g) puy lentils
3 tablespoons extra virgin
    olive oil
2 golden shallots, chopped
1 clove garlic, finely chopped
2 anchovy fillets
1 carrot, chopped
1 celery stick, chopped
6–7 marjoram leaves
salt flakes and freshly ground
    black pepper
1 yellow capsicum (pepper),
    seeds and membrane
    removed, cut into strips
1 red capsicum (pepper), seeds
    and membrane removed,
    cut into strips
4–5 roma (plum) tomatoes,
    peeled, seeded and chopped
2 tablespoons red wine vinegar
flat-leaf parsley leaves,
    to garnish

1   Rinse the lentils under cold water to get rid of any grit, then drain and set aside.

2   Heat the olive oil in a medium saucepan over medium heat, add the shallot, garlic and anchovies and cook for 1 minute or until the garlic smells fragrant and the anchovies have melted into the oil. Add the carrot and celery and cook over low–medium heat for 1–2 minutes, then stir in the lentils, marjoram and a pinch of salt. Pour in enough water to cover the lentils and bring to a simmer, then reduce the heat to low and cook, covered, for 30 minutes. Check the water level during this time and add a little more if needed to keep the lentils covered.

3   Remove the lid and add the capsicum, tomato and a little water to keep everything submerged. Cook for 20 minutes or until the lentils have absorbed the liquid and are cooked through and the capsicum strips have softened. Season to taste with salt and pepper and stir in the vinegar, then top with a few parsley leaves and serve warm or at room temperature.

•   *Puy lentils work so well in this recipe because they hold their shape during cooking and keep a slight al dente bite. They are small and dark brown, with a slight blue tinge, and have a savoury, peppery flavour.*

CECI in UMIDO

• CHICKPEA STEW •

Although it is true that most Italians would happily live on pasta al pomodoro or veal saltimbocca most days of their lives, it is a lesser known fact that everyday Italian food can happily accommodate the latest nutritional trends: from the gluten intolerant to the ethical vegan. Vegetables and pulses feature prominently in most regional cuisines in a vast array of delicious presentations. Chickpeas are often used in Italian cooking, from chickpea bread (farinata) to chickpea soup (pasta e ceci). In Molise they love to stew them with onion, garlic and a good dash of the local fiery chilli, diavolillo. If you are using dried chickpeas, they will need to soak overnight so start the recipe a day ahead.

SERVES 4 AS A SIDE DISH

2 cups (400 g) dried chickpeas
 or 2 × 400 g tins chickpeas,
 well drained
3 tablespoons extra virgin
 olive oil, plus extra
 for drizzling
1 small chunk of pancetta
 or speck (omit for
 a vegetarian option)
1 piece pecorino or
 parmigiano rind
4–5 spring onions,
 thinly sliced
1–2 bay leaves
1 clove garlic, finely chopped
1 diavolillo or any hot
 chilli you can find,
 finely chopped
1 litre chicken or
 vegetable stock
salt flakes

1   If you are using dried chickpeas, soak them in water overnight, changing the water once or twice. Drain, then place the soaked chickpeas in a saucepan and cover with water. Simmer for 45–60 minutes or until tender. Drain and set aside until ready to use.

2   Heat the olive oil in a medium heavy-based saucepan over medium heat, add the pancetta or speck, cheese rind, spring onion and bay leaves and cook for 1–2 minutes, then add the garlic and chilli and cook for 1 minute or until fragrant. Add the drained chickpeas, cover with stock and simmer for 15–20 minutes or until the stock has reduced by one third. Taste for salt and adjust accordingly.

3   Serve as a side dish, or enjoy it on its own, drizzled with peppery extra virgin olive oil.

• *Chickpeas are a great iron boost. Make sure you include them on your shopping list when you are feeling run down or overworked.*

The local dialect of Molise is very similar to Abruzzese, a clear sign of the intertwined cultures of the two regions. It sounds ancient and intriguing and is rich with funny little proverbs. Here are a few examples of the intricacy of this language that can sound obscure to most northern Italians.

Molisano: A gatte ferejose a fatt 'i fijje cecate
(A cat in a hurry makes blind kittens)
English: A job done in a hurry is
a job poorly done

Molisano: U fesse parle sembe
(The fool never shuts up)
English: The fool is never quiet

Molisano: Chi spèra a re luòtte, sta sembe
a pancuotte (If you rely on Lotto,
you end up eating bread soup)
English: You can't rely on luck

ZUPPA di CIPOLLE

◆ ONION STEW ◆

The Molisani are so devoted to their onions that they have dedicated a food festival to them. Every year on 29 June the main square of Isernia is transformed into the setting of this famous festival, attracting local producers to show off the magnificent fruits of their labour. The most celebrated variety, the bulbous red onion, makes a spectacular stew that certainly gives the notable French dish a run for its money. However, if you are unable to find a basket of freshly plucked Molisane red onions at your local store, the more readily available Spanish (red) onion or the good-old brown onion will make a dignified replacement. Serve this with a lovely red wine, such as Montepulciano d'Abruzzo or Tintilia.

SERVES 4–6

4–5 tablespoons extra virgin olive oil
8 red onions, thinly sliced
1–2 sprigs thyme
salt flakes and freshly ground white pepper
pinch of sugar
2 tablespoons vin cotto (see Note)
3 litres good chicken stock
toasted bread, to serve

1 Heat the olive oil in a large heavy-based saucepan over medium–high heat, add the onion, thyme and a pinch of salt, then reduce the heat to low–medium and cook for 8–10 minutes, stirring gently, until the onion is soft and translucent. Add the sugar and vin cotto and cook for another 2–3 minutes, then cover with a lid and cook over low heat for 10–15 minutes.

2 Pour in the stock and simmer, uncovered, for 35–40 minutes or until the soup has thickened slightly and reduced by one third. Be sure to stir it occasionally to prevent it from sticking. Taste for salt and adjust accordingly, then season with pepper and serve hot with toasted spelt ciabatta (see page 20) or any crusty bread you love.

◆ *If vin cotto is hard to find at your local store, you can use balsamic vinegar or verjuice instead.*

TAGLIOLINI *ai* RICCI *di* MARE

• HOMEMADE TAGLIOLINI WITH SEA URCHIN ROE •

When I was little, we enjoyed a family holiday in Termoli, a gorgeous coastal town in Molise. We frolicked in the warm Mediterranean water, strolled around the narrow cobblestone streets savouring gelato and, come nightfall, we'd be amongst the first securing a table at the local seafood restaurants. Papá, a serious buon gustaio (foodie), would never bother consulting the menu. He'd simply ask the waiter 'Ce li hai i ricci?' (Do you have sea urchin?) If the answer was 'si', Papá would simply wink and a superb platter of this fresh pasta would soon be on its way.

SERVES 4

4 tablespoons extra virgin
   olive oil
1 clove garlic, finely chopped
2 tablespoons finely chopped
   flat-leaf parsley stalks
1 small chilli, thinly sliced
250 g sea urchin roe
150 ml white wine
salt flakes
finely grated zest of 1 lemon
flat-leaf parsley leaves,
   to garnish

TAGLIOLINI
2⅔ cups (400 g) plain flour
4 eggs
1 scant teaspoon salt flakes
semolina flour, for dusting

1 To make the tagliolini dough, place the flour on a wooden board, make a well in the centre and drop in the eggs and salt. Mix together using your fingers or a fork, then knead vigorously for about 10 minutes. At first it will look crumbly, but once your body heat activates the starch in the flour the dough will change its texture, transforming into a smooth, firm ball. (If you want to speed things up you can mix the dough ingredients in a food processor until they resemble wet sand, then tip onto a floured board, bring together with your hands and knead for 1 minute.) Wrap the dough in plastic film and let it rest in the fridge for 30 minutes.

2 Cut the dough into quarters. Work with one piece at a time and keep the rest wrapped in plastic film to prevent it from drying out. Flatten the piece of dough with the palm of your hand, then pass it through the pasta machine's widest setting three or four times, folding the dough into three each time. Continue passing the dough, each time through a thinner setting, until you get to the second-last setting or the sheet is roughly 2.5 mm thick. If you don't have a pasta machine, you can use a rolling pin and a lot of elbow grease.

3 Pass the pasta sheets through the spaghetti/tagliolini cutter of your pasta machine. Gently place the cut noodles on a floured tea towel, dust with semolina and allow to dry slightly at room temperature. If you are in a very hot climate, place the pasta in the fridge until you are ready to cook it.

4 Bring a large saucepan of salted water to the boil while you make the sauce.

• *Wrap any leftover pasta dough in plastic film and store it in the fridge, where it will keep for up to 2 days.*

5 Heat the olive oil in a large heavy-based frying pan over medium heat. Add the garlic, parsley stalks and chilli and cook for 1 minute or until the garlic starts to turn pale golden. Add the roe and cook in the flavoured oil for 1 minute, then pour in the wine and cook over high heat for 1–2 minutes or until the alcohol has evaporated. Turn off the heat, taste for salt and adjust to your liking.

6 When the water comes to the boil, drop in your tagliolini and cook for 2–3 minutes or until al dente. Drain, reserving 3–4 tablespoons of the cooking water. Heat up the sauce, add the cooked pasta and toss to combine. If it is too dry, add some of the reserved pasta water. Serve hot dusted with freshly grated lemon zest and a scattering of parsley leaves.

I POLPE 'NPERGATORI

• OCTOPUS IN PURGATORY (AKA SPICY BABY OCTOPUS STEW) •

I really think the Molisani ought to rename this dish 'Octopus in hell'! It really packs a punch! Something mysterious happens after you have endured that first spicy bite – as your palate adapts to the intensity of the punch and your brain releases endorphins through your body, the melting texture of the octopus combined with the rich, mellow flavour of the wine sauce will envelop your senses in a warm embrace that will linger. It will make you reach for a second helping, and a third . . .

SERVES 4

4 tablespoons extra virgin
    olive oil
1 red onion, thinly sliced
1 clove garlic, finely chopped
1–2 teaspoons chilli flakes
    (use as much as you
    can handle!)
1 kg baby octopus, cleaned
    (see Note)
200 ml red wine
200 ml water
salt flakes
crusty bread, to serve

1 Heat the olive oil in a large heavy-based frying pan over medium heat, add the onion and cook for 1–2 minutes or until softened. Add the garlic and chilli flakes and cook for another 1–2 minutes. Add the octopus and stir-fry for 2–3 minutes, then pour in the wine and cook for 1–2 minutes or until the alcohol has evaporated. Add the water and bring to a simmer, then cover with a lid and cook over low heat for 1–1½ hours or until the octopus is tender. Taste for salt and adjust accordingly.

2 Serve hot with chunks of bread to mop up that glorious sauce.

• *To clean baby octopus, take a small sharp knife and cut the heads off. Clean out the guts and rinse under cold water to remove any grit. Gently push your thumbs through the middle part of the body to extract the beak.*

CROSTACEI ALL' AGRO

• CRUSTACEA WITH LEMON, GARLIC AND PARSLEY SAUCE •

The fortunate geographical position of Molise is one of the secrets behind such interesting and varied regional dishes, ranging from slow-cooked sheep (typical of the mountains), stuffed vegetables from the sweeping, verdant valleys and the truly exceptional fruits of the Adriatic Sea. Seafood is always cooked simply, often merely drizzled with lemon, parsley and olive oil.

Pannocchie (or cicale di mare), a variety of mantis shrimp, are typical of these waters, and are best eaten in winter when the flesh is rich and succulent. The ancient-looking Balmain bug is its closest approximation and can be used in this recipe if pannocchie are hard to come by, as can scampi or langoustines.

SERVES 4

8 Balmain or Moreton Bay
    bugs (or 1 kg pannocchie)
juice of 1 lemon
1 clove garlic, very finely
    chopped
3–4 tablespoons finely
    chopped flat-leaf parsley
3 tablespoons extra virgin
    olive oil
salt flakes and freshly ground
    white pepper

1   Start by preparing the bugs. In order to easily separate the flesh from the shell, bring a large saucepan of water to the boil, add the bugs and cook for 5 minutes.

2   Meanwhile, to make a dressing, whisk together the lemon juice, garlic, parsley, 2 tablespoons olive oil and a pinch of salt and pepper.

3   Remove the bugs from the pan and leave to cool for 5 minutes. Flip them tummy-side up and, using kitchen scissors, cut the shell open lengthways. Pull the flesh out – you will notice that it is only partially cooked. Not for long! Wipe the pan with paper towel, then add the remaining olive oil and cook the bug meat over medium heat for 2–3 minutes.

4   Place the bug meat on a serving platter, drizzle with the dressing and serve straight away as a magnificent starter.

• *You can also use the dressing to drizzle over steamed white fish such as snapper or sea bass.*

Signora Antonietta
in Campobasso

Happy goats and sheep roaming in the green valleys of Molise

RAGÙ di CAPRA con MALEFANTE

• FRESH PASTA STRIPS WITH SLOW-COOKED GOAT SAUCE •

Goat meat is very popular in the peasant cooking tradition of central Italy. Whether the choice falls to the delicately flavoured kid or the slightly gamey chevon, Molisani home cooks seem to agree that it is as versatile as lamb and offers just as much nutritional value, but with less fat and cholesterol. One of the best ways to enjoy it is to slow-braise it until you are left with tender, sweet and succulent meat that falls off the bone, enveloped in a rich wine and tomato sauce, ready to mingle with malefante, a durum wheat pasta typical of Molise.

SERVES 6

4–5 tablespoons extra virgin olive oil
6 goat forequarter chops
4 cloves garlic, skin removed, bashed with the palm of your hand
2 carrots, chopped
¼ green capsicum (pepper) in 1 piece
2–3 bay leaves
5–6 white peppercorns, crushed
2–3 cloves, crushed
200 ml red wine
2 × 400 g tins tomatoes
400 ml water
1–2 sprigs rosemary
1 small piece pecorino rind
salt flakes
grated pecorino, to serve

MALEFANTE
3 cups (450 g) durum wheat flour, specialty pasta flour or plain flour, plus extra for dusting
pinch of salt flakes
250–300 ml warm water
olive oil, for greasing your hands
semolina flour, for dusting

1 Heat the olive oil in a large heavy-based saucepan over medium–high heat and brown the goat chops. Add the garlic, carrot and capsicum and cook for 4–5 minutes, then add the bay leaves, peppercorns and cloves. Pour in the wine to deglaze the pan and cook over high heat for 2–3 minutes or until the alcohol has evaporated.

2 Add the tomatoes and water. Bring to a simmer, then reduce the heat to low and add the rosemary sprigs, pecorino rind and a pinch of salt. Cover with a lid and leave to cook gently for 3–4 hours or until the meat falls off the bones and the sauce is rich and a deep crimson. Take out the goat chops and remove the meat from the bones. Break up the meat with a fork – it will show no resistance. Remove and discard the garlic cloves, capsicum and cheese rind, then return the goat meat to the pan. Taste for salt and adjust accordingly.

3 Meanwhile, to make the malefante, put the flour and salt in a large mixing bowl, make a well in the centre, then slowly pour in the water, mixing as you go with a chopstick or your finger. Don't add all the water at once as you may not need it all. I would suggest you start with 250 ml and add the rest if needed. As a rule of thumb, a dry dough is easier to correct than a tacky one. Mix until the dough resembles wet crumbs, then tip it onto a floured surface, oil your hands and knead it for 3–4 minutes or until it comes together in a smooth ball. Cover it in plastic film and let it rest in the fridge for 30 minutes. You can make the dough a day ahead if you like. (If you have a food processor, you can use it to get this dough together in less then 2 minutes and with minimum mess. It should only need a minute or so of kneading until smooth.)

- *If you are short of time, you can buy fresh pappardelle and cut them into strips. No judgement, I promise. I have done it myself many, many times.*

4 Using a rolling pin or a pasta machine, roll out the dough to a thickness of 3 mm, then cut it into 8 cm × 2 cm strips (give or take!). Dust them with flour so they won't stick together and lay on a large platter or board dusted with semolina flour.

5 Shortly before the sauce is ready, bring a large saucepan of salted water to the boil and cook the pasta for 3–4 minutes or until al dente. Drain, but be sure to reserve 2–3 tablespoons of the cooking water to add to the sauce.

6 Toss the pasta with the sauce, add some or all of the reserved cooking water, if needed, and serve hot, dusted with pecorino.

CAVATELLI LUNGHI *alla* MOLISANA

• HANDMADE PASTA WITH SLOW-COOKED MEAT SAUCE •

In the best tradition of regional cuisine, you can travel around Molise and never taste the same dish bearing this name. I have been confounded by offerings of homemade pasta tossed in a sauce meat had been cooked in, but no remnants of any beast were to be found on my plate. A closer look at the menu would reveal a second course of carne al sugo (meat cooked in tomato sauce). Ah . . . There is my protein! On other occasions, the noodles themselves might come shaped as long fusilli or small gnocchi. So take this recipe as one version only. I can swear this is the way I had it in Campobasso, but who knows how they dish it up in the neighbouring town of Isernia? Fundamentally, this is fresh pasta with a slow-cooked meat sauce. Put your twist on it and if anyone asks, tell them this is just how they make it in the charming village of Capracotta. See if they argue! *Pictured page 256.*

SERVES 4

4 tablespoons extra virgin olive oil

300 g Italian pork and fennel sausage, casings removed

5–6 × 2 cm thick pork rashers, cut into thirds

400 g lamb stewing pieces (such as leg steaks or shoulder chops)

1 carrot, roughly chopped

1 onion, roughly chopped

1 celery stick, roughly chopped

1 clove garlic, chopped

200 ml red wine

2 × 400 g tins tomatoes

400 ml water

salt flakes

freshly grated or shaved pecorino, to serve

CAVATELLI LUNGHI

2 cups (300 g) durum wheat flour, plain flour or specialty pasta flour, plus extra for dusting

1 teaspoon salt flakes

220–250 ml lukewarm water

1 Heat 3 tablespoons olive oil in a large flameproof casserole dish over medium heat. Add all the meats and brown well all over. Remove to a plate. Heat the remaining oil in the casserole and cook the carrot, onion, celery and garlic until they smell fragrant. Return the meat to the casserole, along with the resting juices, and cook together for 1–2 minutes, then pour in the wine and cook for 1–2 minutes or until the alcohol has evaporated. Add the tomatoes, water and a pinch of salt and bring to a simmer, then reduce the heat to low and cook, covered, for 2–3 hours, stirring occasionally. After that time, taste for salt and adjust to your liking. If the sauce is too liquid, increase the heat and let it boil for 5–10 minutes or until reduced and thickened. Remove the meat and break it up to remove any bones. Put the meat back in the sauce.

2 While the sauce is cooking, make the cavatelli lunghi. Put the flour and salt in a large mixing bowl, make a well in the centre and slowly pour in the water, mixing as you go to incorporate the flour. Don't add all the water at once as you may not need it all, depending on the brand of flour you use; by the same token, you may need to add a little extra water if the dough is too stiff or dry. Using 100% durum wheat flour will probably require a little more liquid than plain or specialty pasta flour.

3 Tip the dough onto a floured surface, oil your hands and knead for 3–4 minutes or until it comes together in a smooth ball. Add a little extra flour if it feels a bit sticky. Wrap it in

• *Don't despair if you can't find the time to make cavatelli from scratch. Casarecce or fusilli will work beautifully – just be sure to cook it to a perfect al dente texture.*

plastic film and let it rest in the fridge for 30 minutes. You can make the dough a day ahead, if it's more convenient. If you do this, take it out of the fridge at least 1 hour before you intend to use it.

4   Take the dough out of the fridge, dust a large wooden board with flour and cut the dough into 6–8 pieces. Rub your hands in olive oil and roll each piece into a long log about 5 mm thick, then cut into 3 cm lengths.

5   Working with one piece of pasta at a time, use a floured butter knife to push it down then drag it towards you to roll your cavatelli and create a slit in the middle, essential for trapping the sauce. Keep going until you have shaped all the cavatelli, then leave them to dry on a wooden board or a wire rack at room temperature.

6   Bring a large saucepan of salted water to the boil, drop in the cavatelli and cook for 5 minutes or until perfectly al dente. Drain, reserving a few tablespoons of the pasta cooking water. Toss the cavatelli in the sauce and warm over medium heat for 1 minute, adding a little pasta cooking water if it is too dry. Serve piping hot, crowned with pecorino.

HANDMADE PASTA WITH SLOW-COOKED MEAT SAUCE (see page 254)

Campobasso dd centre

AGNELLO *in* BRODO *con* PISELLI *e* FAVE

• LAMB IN BROTH WITH PEAS AND BROAD BEANS •

Is this a lamb stew with greens or a pea and broad bean soup with flaky, slow-cooked meat? The answer to this impossible question is irrelevant, as this modest combination of ingredients produces a dish that is at once hearty and delicate, which celebrates spring with every luscious mouthful, whatever name you wish to give it.

SERVES 4

4 tablespoons extra virgin olive oil

4 lamb shanks

2–3 cloves garlic, skin removed, bashed with the palm of your hand

4–5 anchovy fillets

150 ml white wine

2 cups (500 ml) chicken or beef stock

2–3 golden shallots, peeled and cut in half

a few oregano leaves

1 cup (120 g) shelled broad beans, skins removed

1 cup (160 g) shelled peas (or use frozen)

salt flakes

a few mint leaves

grated zest of 1 lemon

crusty bread, to serve (optional)

1 Heat 2 tablespoons olive oil in a flameproof casserole dish over medium–high heat and brown the lamb for 3–4 minutes or until evenly browned. Remove from the pan and set aside. Add the remaining oil, garlic and anchovies and cook for 1–2 minutes, stirring the anchovies with a fork to encourage them to melt into the oil.

2 Return the lamb to the dish, pour in the wine and cook over high heat for 2–3 minutes or until the alcohol has evaporated. Pour in the stock and add the shallot and oregano leaves. Bring to a simmer, then reduce the heat to low and cook, covered, for 2–3 hours or until the lamb is very tender.

3 Take the lid off, add the broad beans and peas and cook over medium heat for 5 minutes or so. Turn off the heat, taste for salt and adjust accordingly (keep in mind that the anchovies are already quite salty).

4 Tear a few mint leaves over the dish, top with lemon zest and serve hot, preferably with a generous amount of bread.

• *For a more substantial dish, boil 300 g ditalini pasta until al dente, then toss it through the stew.*

LA PEZZATA

• SHEEP STEW •

The origin of this dish dates back to the days when transhumance, the traditional movement of sheep and cows from the highlands to the lowlands, was common practice in Abruzzo and Molise. Should a sheep become crippled during the journey, it would become dinner for the shepherds. The animal would be chopped into 'pezzato' (pieces) and stewed with a few other simple ingredients, whatever was available on such a long and hard expedition. In a culinary twist of fate, pezzata has gone from an emergency dish for cowboys from Molise to a delicacy for 'buon gustai' (gourmands) and those attached to ancient traditions, and has an entire food festival devoted to it. The original recipe suggests you boil the meat gently for 4–5 hours, skimming off the impurities that gradually come to the surface and replacing the boiling liquid once during that time. This practice is necessary when cooking an animal that is past its prime and has acquired a rather tough texture and gamey flavour. These days it is much easier to find meat that comes from a younger animal and all that is left for you to do is to stew it gently as you would with lamb or goat.

SERVES 4–6

3 tablespoons extra virgin
   olive oil
1 kg sheep meat (shank,
   shoulder or leg), trimmed
   and cut into large chunks
2 carrots, cut into 3 pieces
2 celery sticks, cut into
   3 pieces
1 brown onion, peeled,
   cut in half and studded
   with 3 cloves
salt flakes
beef stock, to cover
3–4 roma (plum) tomatoes,
   peeled and cut into
   quarters
4–5 potatoes, peeled and
   cut into quarters
handful of mixed herbs
   (such as marjoram,
   oregano or rosemary)
1 teaspoon chilli flakes
4–6 thick slices bread

1 Heat the olive oil in a large flameproof casserole dish over medium heat. Brown the meat in batches, then add the carrot, celery and onion, season with salt and pour in enough stock to cover the meat. Bring to a simmer, then cover and cook over low heat for 2 hours. Skim off any excess fat that has come to the surface, then add the tomato, potato, herbs and chilli flakes and cook, covered, for a further 45–60 minutes or until the flesh is fork tender.

2 Take the lid off and cook over medium–high heat for about 5 minutes to slightly reduce the sauce. Taste for salt and adjust accordingly, then remove from the heat.

3 Grill the bread on both sides. Ladle the stew into bowls and serve with a slice of grilled bread.

• *Unsurprisingly, pezzata is even better the next day, served with grilled bread or soft polenta (see page 59).*

Life in the streets of Campobasso

There are many delectable varieties of preserved meat and dairy products that are an essential part of a Molisano antipasti spread. These include ventricina, liver sausage, torciniello (a lamb offal sausage), buffalo mozzarella from Venafro, pecorino and burrino, a butter-filled cheese.

MOSTACCIOLI

◆ HONEY, CHOCOLATE AND NUTMEG COOKIES ◆

Mostaccioli owe their name to one of the ingredients they are made with: grape must (mosto). These days, this elusive ingredient has been replaced with a combination of cocoa, spices and vin cotto, but these cookies still remain very popular in Molise and indeed all of southern Italy, with each region battling it out for the best recipe. Traditionally made to herald the Christmas festivities, mostaccioli are now enjoyed all year round, and are the perfect excuse to indulge in a glass of amaro or vin santo to dunk them in.

MAKES 40

3 tablespoons extra virgin
    olive oil
200 g honey
100 g caster sugar
1 tablespoon vin cotto
50 g dark chocolate chips
2 tablespoons dutch cocoa
    powder (see Note)
2 teaspoons ground cinnamon
1 teaspoon ground cloves
finely grated zest of ½ orange
130 g toasted ground almonds
2 cups (300 g) self-raising flour
250 g dark chocolate, broken
    into pieces

1 Place the olive oil, honey, sugar, vin cotto and chocolate chips in a medium saucepan and stir over low–medium heat for 2–3 minutes. Add the cocoa powder, spices and orange zest and mix to combine, then turn off the heat. Stir in the ground almonds, then gradually add the flour until a dough is formed.

2 Line a large baking tray with baking paper. Tip the dough onto the tray and gently flatten out to a 5 mm thick rectangle. Rest in the fridge for 30 minutes to allow it to firm up. (Make sure you wash the pan and any utensils you used to make the dough *straight away* otherwise the combination of honey, melted sugar and chocolate will prove extremely difficult to remove. Alas, I know from experience!)

3 Preheat your oven to 190°C (170°C fan-forced) and line another large baking tray with baking paper.

4 Take the tray out of the fridge and cut the dough into 4 cm diamonds. Arrange them on the prepared tray, leaving plenty of room for spreading. Bake for 18–20 minutes or until cooked through but still slightly soft. They will firm up to a crunchy texture as they cool down. Cool on the tray for a few minutes, then transfer to a wire rack and cool for 2–3 hours.

5 Melt the chocolate in a heatproof bowl set over a saucepan of barely simmering water, stirring occasionally (make sure the bowl doesn't touch the water). Dip the top of each biscuit into the molten chocolate, then place on a wire rack to cool and set. Mostaccioli will keep well in an airtight container for 3–4 days and make a delightful edible Christmas gift.

◆ *If dutch cocoa powder is unavailable, regular dark cocoa powder
will work just as well.*

PESCHE *di* CASTELBOTTACCIO

• SPONGE CAKES FROM CASTELBOTTACCIO •

Just when you thought you could safely associate Molise with bold, earthy, rich flavours, enter a platter of blushing, soft sponge cakes, flavoured with liqueur and glued together with luscious patisserie cream to resemble the shape of peaches. Mamma made a huge platter of these delicate offerings for my Holy Communion day, intending to serve them to the adults attending the festivities. But my cousins and I were too quick and gulped them down in a heartbeat, unaware that they had been generously lacquered with crimson alchermes liqueur! No wonder my memories of the day I first received the body of Christ are slightly fuzzy . . .

MAKES 10

2 eggs
⅔ cup (150 g) caster sugar
80 g softened butter,
    cut into cubes
2⅔ cups (400 g) self-raising
    flour, sifted
1 teaspoon vanilla paste
    or extract
1 cup (250 ml) alchermes
    liqueur (see Note)
1 cup (220 g) caster sugar,
    extra
tiny mint leaves, to garnish

CUSTARD
2 cups (500 ml) milk
rind of 1 lemon, in strips
1 vanilla bean, split in half,
    seeds scraped
4 egg yolks
4 tablespoons caster sugar
40 g cornflour

1   Preheat your oven to 170°C (150°C fan-forced). Line a large baking tray with baking paper.

2   Cream the eggs and sugar until pale and frothy, then add the butter, a little at a time, and beat well – you can either do this in a bowl with a wooden spoon or use a stand mixer (my favourite toy!). Gradually add the flour and vanilla until your batter reaches a dropping consistency. Dollop large walnut-sized balls of batter onto the prepared baking tray, leaving plenty of room for spreading. Bake for 18–20 minutes or until pale golden and cooked through. Cool on the tray for a few minutes, then transfer to a wire rack to cool completely.

3   In the meantime, make the custard. Heat the milk in a medium saucepan and bring to just below simmering. Remove from the heat, then add the lemon rind and vanilla and leave to infuse for 10 minutes. In a medium bowl, beat the egg yolks and sugar until pale and fluffy. You can do this by hand using a whisk or with hand-held electric beaters. Add the cornflour and mix with a wooden spoon until combined.

4   Strain the infused milk, then gently pour it into the egg mixture, whisking constantly until smooth and well combined. Pour the mixture back into the saucepan and bring to a gentle simmer, stirring constantly. Reduce the heat to low and cook, stirring, for 3–4 minutes or until it becomes thick and luscious. Pour the custard into a bowl and cover the surface with plastic film so it doesn't form a skin. If you're not using it straight away, allow it to cool at room temperature, then transfer it to the fridge, where it will keep for up to 2 days.

• *If alchermes is hard to come by or a little too extravagant for your taste, ruby-red Campari will make a suitable replacement.*

5 Using a teaspoon, scoop out a little bit from the bottom of each cake to accommodate the filling. Fill the indents with custard, then sandwich with another mini cake.

6 Pour the alchermes into a bowl and tip the extra sugar into another bowl. Dip the sandwiched cakes into the liqueur, then roll them in the sugar and arrange them on a plate. Decorate the cakes with mint leaves and serve.

TORTA di NOCI e CIOCCOLATO

• FLOURLESS WALNUT CAKE •

I am really thrilled to get my hands on this ancient recipe (it dates back to 1894!). This is a wonderfully rich and moist cake that contains, believe it or not, no gluten and no butter. The most ardent nutritionist would have to approve of Pellegrino Artusi's recipe, which is included in his impressive work, *Science in the Kitchen and the Art of Eating Well*. To be honest, Mr Artusi doesn't specify where this cake originated from, but having admired and tasted similar puddings all around Molise, I have a feeling it may well come from these parts. I have tweaked the recipe ever so slightly in order to make it more user-friendly and to infuse it with a little Christmas spirit.

SERVES 10–12

2½ cups (250 g) walnuts
1 cup (220 g) brown sugar
250 g dark chocolate, cut into small chunks
6 eggs
1 teaspoon ground cinnamon
½ teaspoon ground cloves
finely grated zest of 1 orange
100 g mixed peel, dusted with flour (use rice or tapioca flour for a gluten-free option)
icing sugar, for dusting

1 Preheat your oven to 180°C (160°C fan-forced). Grease and flour a 24 cm round cake tin.

2 Place the walnuts and brown sugar in a food processor and pulse six to eight times or until the walnuts are crushed, but not pulverised. Add the chocolate and pulse another two or three times. (Pellegrino Artusi's recipe calls for a fair bit of elbow grease, as a food processor wasn't exactly a kitchen essential back in the 1890s. He suggests you prepare the nuts with a rolling pin and the chocolate with a grater . . . go for it, if you fancy a little workout in the kitchen!) Add the eggs, cinnamon and cloves and mix to combine, then mix in the orange zest and mixed peel.

3 Pour the batter into the prepared tin and bake for 35–40 minutes. The cake should be slightly cracked around the edges and the middle should feel soft and bouncy. As it cools, it will firm up further. Cool in the tin for 20 minutes, then transfer to a wire rack to cool completely. Dust liberally with icing sugar and serve thin slices with coffee or amaro liqueur.

• *This cake keeps well for 4–5 days, stored in an airtight container, and tends to improve in flavour and texture after a day or two.*

TORTA di MELE DELLA SIGNORA PIA

• SIGNORA PIA'S APPLE CAKE •

Travelling around Italy with theatre shows in the early noughties gave me the invaluable gift of experiencing first hand the marvels and variety of regional cuisine. However, one of the many things thespians have in common the world over is a meagre wage, so I quickly became very thrifty with quite a sophisticated radar for cheap deals, such as the local 3-star, family-run pensione that would also offer food at a reasonable price. More often than not, the cuisine was exquisitely simple and delicious.

This rustic apple cake takes me straight back to Isernia, to the very tiny room I shared with three noisy castmates (we were musical theatre performers, after all!) and the enticing aromas coming from Signora Pia's kitchen. Breakfast was always a favourite, especially when she'd bake this cinnamon-perfumed cake, with apple rounds slowly sinking into the fluffy batter around them. Admittedly, this is not her recipe word for word, but the essence is there, and I find myself catapulted back to those bohemian days with each and every mouthful.

SERVES 8

3 eggs, separated
130 g caster sugar
4 tablespoons extra virgin
  olive oil
150 ml pouring cream
pinch of salt flakes
finely grated zest of 1 lemon
1 teaspoon ground cinnamon,
  plus extra for dusting
  (optional)
1½ cups (225 g) self-raising
  flour, sifted
1 large or 2 small apples
  (such as pink lady, royal
  gala or golden delicious),
  peeled, cored and cut into
  3–4 mm thick rounds

1 Preheat your oven to 180°C (160°C fan-forced). Grease and flour a 24 cm round cake tin.

2 Place the egg yolks and sugar in a mixing bowl and beat vigorously until pale and fluffy. Add the olive oil, cream, salt, lemon zest and cinnamon and combine well. Slowly add the flour and mix well to incorporate it into the batter, but don't beat it too hard or the cake will become a little dense.

3 Beat the egg whites with a pinch of salt to form soft peaks, then gently fold into the batter.

4 Pour the batter into the prepared tin and arrange the apple rounds on top. As the cake bakes it will puff up, enveloping the apple slices in its delicate embrace.

5 Bake for 35–40 minutes or until a skewer inserted into the middle of the cake comes out clean. Remove from the oven and cool in the tin for at least an hour before serving. Enjoy it just as it is, or dusted with extra cinnamon, with a cup of tea or coffee.

• *Signora Pia's cake will keep moist and fresh for up to 3 days wrapped in foil or stored in an airtight container at room temperature.*

Dried oregano at
Campobasso farmers' market

Exploring Pietrabbondante

Pietrabbondante, Molise

ACKNOWLEDGEMENTS

◆ ◆ ◆ ◆ ◆ ◆ ◆

When trying to express my gratitude for the endless help and support I was given throughout this project, words simply don't suffice. So, instead of a long list of 'thank yous', I am sending out virtual food gifts to everyone who has been there for me.

To my amazing team at Penguin Australia – the talented Evi O, Rachel Carter, Daniel New and Katrina O'Brien – I would like to celebrate with a gargantuan feast of freshly made maccheroni alla chitarra with saffron and zucchini blossoms.

To Chris Chen, whose brilliant food photography made my recipes come to life, I will be making my brother's vongole and chickpea pasta. I seem to remember you enjoyed it on the day!

To the ladies who made my food look so pretty – the lovely Cass Stokes and the energetic Jane Hann – I am making a large batch of tozzetti cookies to devour with generous helpings of gelato. You deserve it!

Jono Fleming, I owe you big time! Your help and efficiency in the kitchen were phenomenal. Basically, pick at random from the index, and I'll cook it for you!

To the unstoppable Julie Gibbs, whose drive and zest for life is infectious, I would like to send a large platter of my nonna's honey-drizzled cluster cake.

To the amazing Carla Coulson, the lady who captured my Italy through such inspired eyes, I will make my gluten-free, dairy-free walnut cake.

To Grace Heifetz and Pippa Masson at Curtis Brown, I am so thankful to be represented by you! Thank you from the bottom of my heart and enjoy my freshly made cavatelli with slow-cooked meat sauce.

I would like to send my team at United Management – Lee-Anne Higgins, Catherine Handley, Natasha Harrison and Trish McAskil – my apricot cake. I am so lucky to be part of the United family!

To Adrian Brant, the FremantleMedia team and SBS Australia, I think you've got yourselves a five-course meal! Thank you for believing in me and my story.

To my bella Mamma, who helped me test recipes in the heat of a Sydney summer, I will make you Nonno's wine-drenched peaches. You deserve a treat! Papá didn't help so much with the cooking, but was always eager to taste and offer his feedback . . . so grab a spoon and enjoy some peaches too.

To all my family and friends who offered to help, offered to eat and occasionally offered to do the dishes, and to those who helped after I shamelessly played the ENMFL (English not my first language) card, I will treat you to a large slice of coffee-infused layer cake. Diet tomorrow!

To all the people I visited in Italy who entrusted me with their recipes I will hand-roll a large batch of gnocchi with zucchini and pecorino cheese.

Lastly, to my angels Richard, Raffi and Miro Rox, the sources of great love in my life, this book only happened because of the support and strength you give me every day. You have my food, my legacy, but most importantly, my heart.

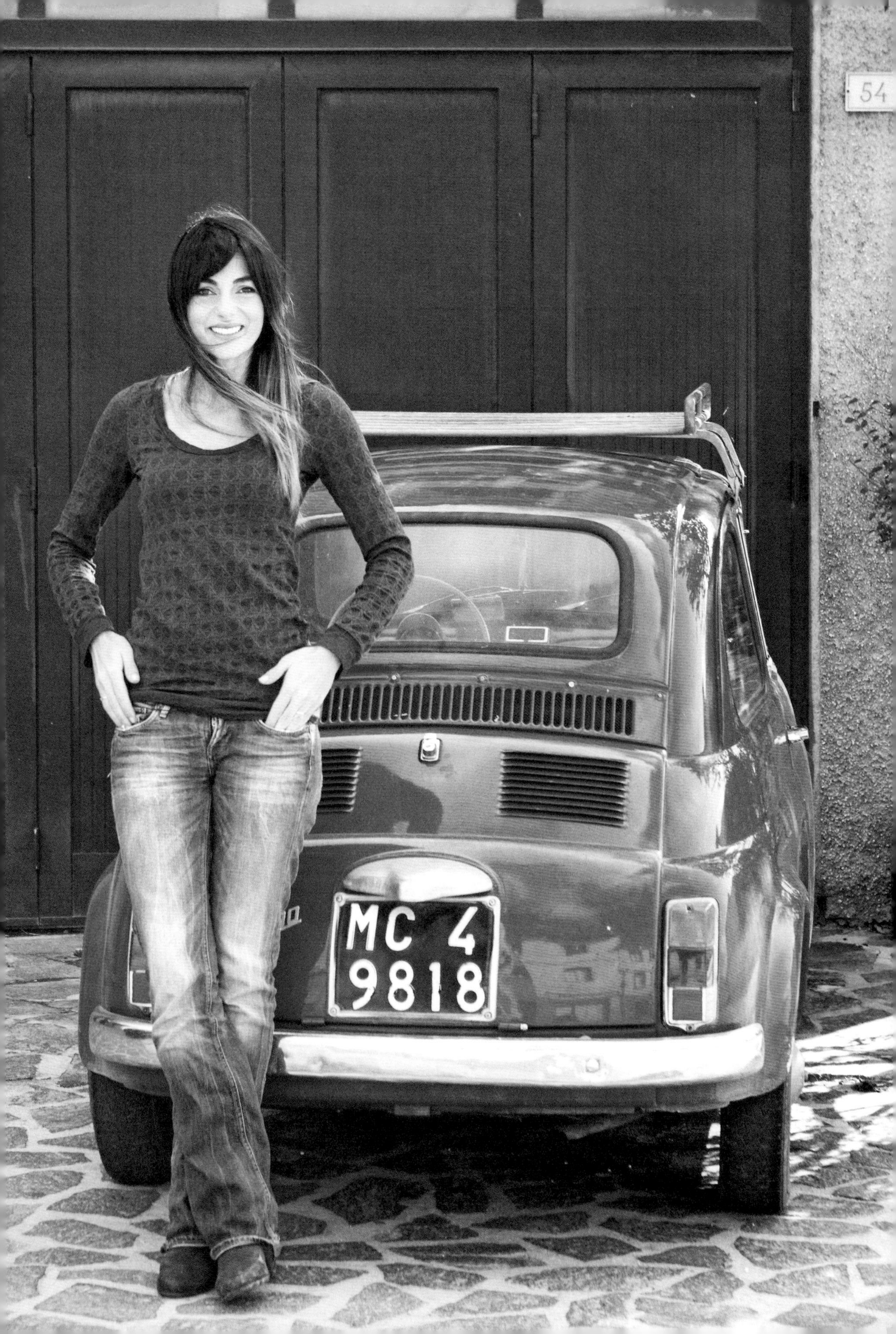
54
MC 4
9818

INDEX

A

Abruzzo 2, 75–193, 196
  cuisines 77
  dairy industry 34
  dialect 173, 240
  digestives 77
  La Presuntuosa 155
  landscapes 77
  Miriam (cousin) 122, 124,
    127, 131
  notable births 95
  pasta 77, 84
  people of 77, 105
  produce 77–8, 186
  recipes 86–188
  Roccascalegna 80, 86
  saffron 174
  San Vito 122–5
  Torricella Peligna 2, 7, 77, 86, 92,
    145, 155, 166, 170, 181
  transhumance 89, 261
  truffles 10, 34
  wines 77
Adamo (Torricella Peligna) 172
Adriatic coastline 137
Agnello alla griglia con asparagi 164
Agnello in brodo con piselli e fave 258
Agnello cacio e ovo 163
agriturismi 60, 152, 163, 164
Agriturismo Troilo 152–5
alchermes liqueur 266, 267
  Celebration sponge cake 182
almonds
  Almond and lemon biscotti 70
  Almond short pastry 224
  Bear's cake 178
  Filled short pastries 176
  toasted and ground 167
anchovies
  Calamari with tomatoes
    and wine 45
antipasti 60, 110, 263
Antonina's cannelloni with
  braised meat 157
apples
  Signora Pia's apple cake 270
Apricot and olive oil cake 66
Arrosticini 159
artichokes
  Artichoke gratin 96, 100
  preparing 96, 99
  preserving colour 102
  Raw artichoke and shaved
    pecorino salad 99
  Sautéed artichokes 102

Artusi, Pellegrino 268
Ascoli Piceno 10
asparagus
  Grilled lamb chops with
    asparagus 164

B

barley
  Cereal soup 150
  in minestrone 33
Battered cauliflower florets 229
beans, dried
  Broccoli rabe and
    borlotti beans 110
  Cereal soup 150
  Pasta and bean soup 148
Bear's cake 178
Béchamel sauce 63
beef
  Lasagne Marche style 10, 62
biga 206
biscuits *see* cookies
Bisnonna Domenica 148
Bocconotti 176
Braised chicken marylands with
  wine and tomatoes 56
bread 18
  Bread pockets with cheese and
    stewed capsicum 114
  Crostini with lemon ricotta and
    spinach 210
  Focaccia with stewed onion 18
  Olive oil bread crescents 206
  pre-ferment 206
  Saint Martin rolls 205
  Spelt ciabatta 12, 20
  Stale bread and pecorino
    dumplings 92
  White wine unleavened bread 86
breadcrumbs
  Artichoke gratin 96, 100
  Gratinated prawns with
    lemon and parsley 40
  making and storing 27
  Stuffed fried olives 10, 22
  Zucchini gratin 27
broad beans
  Lamb in broth with peas and
    broad beans 258
Broccoli rabe and borlotti beans 110
Broccolini cooked with
  chilli and garlic 232
Broccolini ripassati 232
Broken pasta and lentil soup 143

broth
  Crepes in broth 144
  Mussels in pepper broth 138
burrino 263

C

cakes
  Apricot and olive oil cake 66
  Bear's cake 178
  Celebration sponge cake 182
  dunking 69
  Flourless walnut cake 268
  Honey-drizzled cluster cake 184
  Lemon and ricotta
    ring cake 69, 77, 181
  parrozzo 178
  potato starch in 182
  Signora Pia's apple cake 270
  Sponge cakes from
    Castelbottaccio 266
  Vincenzo's fiadone cake 181
  see also cheesecakes
calamari
  Calamari with tomatoes
    and wine 45
  cleaning 45
  Crispy fried prawns and
    calamari 39
Calamari in guazzetto 45
Calcionetti 170
Calzoni con caciocavallo e peperonata 114
Campobasso 5, 196, 209, 257, 262, 272
Cannelloni di Antonina 157
Capè restaurant 148
Capracotta 254
Caprafico 193
caprino *see* goat's curd cheese
capsicum
  Bread pockets with
    cheese and stewed
    capsicum 114
  Lentil and capsicum salad 237
  Stuffed capsicum 230
  Sweet and sour capsicum 112
Carciofi in padella 102
Castellino del Biferno 196, 202
cauliflower
  Battered cauliflower
    florets 229
cavatelli lunghi 254
Cavatelli lunghi alla molisana 254
Ceci in umido 238
Celebration sponge cake 182
Celli pieni 166

Centerbe 176
Cereal soup 150
chard
   Savoury tart with chard 108
cheese 34
   Bread pockets with cheese and
     stewed capsicum 114
   burrino 263
   Egg, lemon and cheese sauce 163
   Grilled primo sale and
     vegetable salad 220
   Homemade primo sale
     cheese 202, 216, 218
   Homemade ricotta 216, 218, 223
   Lamb with egg, lemon and
     cheese sauce 163
   mozzarella 263
   Potato gnocchi with zucchini
     and pecorino 28
   Primo sale 216, 218
   Raw artichoke and shaved
     pecorino salad 99
   scamorza 157, 227
   Stale bread and pecorino
     dumplings 92
   whey 216, 223
   Zucchini gratin 27
cheesecakes
   Lemon and ricotta ring cake
     69, 77, 181
   Vincenzo's fiadone cake 181
cherries
   Ricotta, chocolate and cherry
     tart 224
chicken
   Braised chicken marylands with
     wine and tomatoes 56
   Stuffed fried olives 10, 22
   Woodsman's chicken 59
chickpeas
   Cereal soup 150
   Chickpea and honey pastries 170
   Chickpea stew 238
   Ditalini with clams and chickpeas,
     cooked risotto-style 140
   soaking 238
chilli
   Broccolini cooked with
     chilli and garlic 232
   Octopus in purgatory
     (aka spicy baby
     octopus stew) 246
Chilli oil 127
chitarra 117, 118
chocolate
   Bear's cake 178
   Chocolate glaze 178
   Filled short pastries 176
   Honey, chocolate and nutmeg
     cookies 264
   Ricotta, chocolate and cherry
     tart 224
Ciabatta di farro 20
Ciambellone di limone e ricotta 69
ciauscolo 34
Cicerchiata 184

cinnamon
   Filled short pastries 176
Civitanova del Sannio 5, 196
clams 10
   Ditalini with clams and chickpeas,
     cooked risotto-style 140
Colloca, Loredana (Mamma) 1, 96,
   107, 122, 143, 166, 170
Colloca, Papà 1, 96, 99, 244
Coniglio in porchetta 10, 54
cookies
   Almond and lemon biscotti 70
   Honey, chocolate and nutmeg
     cookies 264
Coratella di agnello 60
cousins
   Miriam 122, 124, 127, 131
   Rosanna 148
Cozze ripiene con chitarrina 128
cream
   Mascarpone cream 188
Crepes in broth 144
Crispy fried prawns and calamari 39
Crostacei all' agro 248
Crostata con ricotta, cioccolato
   e ciliege 224
Crostini con ricotta e spinaci 210
Crostini with lemon ricotta and
   spinach 210
crumbed dishes see breadcrumbs
Crustacea with lemon, garlic and
   parsley sauce 248
cucina povera 60, 196
Custard 266
   Celebration sponge cake
     filling 182
   Saffron custard 174
   Sponge cakes from
     Castelbottaccio 266

D

Di Cino family 181
Di Sangro family 122, 170
digestives 77
Ditalini risottati con vongole e ceci 140
Ditalini with clams and chickpeas,
   cooked risotto-style 140
dumplings
   Stale bread and pecorino
     dumplings 92

E

eggs
   Egg, lemon and cheese sauce 163
   and truffles 34
   see also frittata

F

Fagioli e rape 110
Fara San Martino 77
farmers' markets 24, 96
farro (spelt) 12
   Cereal soup 150

fecola di patate
   (potato starch) 182, 183
ferratelle 90
Fiadone di Vincenzo 77, 181
Filled short pastries 176
first communion 166
fish
   Handmade noodles with
     monkfish ragù 10, 42
   Homemade pasta squares
     with fish stew 126
   Monkfish ragù 10, 42
Flourless walnut cake 268
focaccia
   Focaccia with stewed onion 18
   toppings 18, 19
Focaccia con cipolle 18
Fresh pasta strips with slow-cooked
   goat sauce 252
frittata
   Herb frittata with goat's curd 107
   with leftover roast potatoes 52
Frittata alle erbe con caprino 107
Fritto misto 10, 39

G

Gamberi gratinati 40
garlic
   Broccolini cooked with
     chilli and garlic 232
   cooking in skin 28
   Lemon, garlic and
     parsley sauce 248
Gessopalena 86
glazes
   Chocolate glaze 178
gnocchi
   Potato gnocchi with zucchini
     and pecorino 28
   potatoes for 28
   rolling 28
Gnocchi con zucchine e pecorino 28
goat
   Slow-cooked goat sauce 252
goat's curd cheese 34
   Herb frittata with goat's
     curd 107
Grape jam crescents 166
grape must 166, 264
gratin
   Artichoke gratin 96, 100
   Gratinated prawns with
     lemon and parsley 40
   Zucchini gratin 27
Grilled lamb chops with
   asparagus 164
Grilled primo sale and
   vegetable salad 220

H

Handmade noodles with
   monkfish ragù 10, 42
Handmade pasta with slow-cooked
   meat sauce 254

herbs
    Herb frittata with goat's curd 107
    Roast potatoes with bay
        leaves and cured
        pork cheek 52
    Sautéed lamb offal 60
    see also parsley
Homemade pasta squares
    with fish stew 126
Homemade primo sale
    cheese 202, 216, 218
Homemade ricotta 216, 218, 223
Homemade spaghetti with stuffed
    mussels 128
Homemade tagliolini with
    sea urchin roe 244
honey
    Bear's cake 178
    Chickpea and honey pastries 170
    Honey, chocolate and nutmeg
        cookies 264
    Honey-drizzled cluster cake 184

I

I polpe'npergatorio 246
I rose ch'à pastella 229
Insalata di carciofi e pecorino 99
Insalata di lenticchie e peperoni 237
Isernia 243, 270

L

La pezzata 261
La Presuntuosa 155
lamb
    Grilled lamb chops with
        asparagus 164
    Handmade pasta with slow-cooked
        meat sauce 254
    Lamb in broth with peas
        and broad beans 258
    Lamb with egg, lemon and
        cheese sauce 163
    Slow-cooked meat sauce 254
    see also sheep's meat
lamb offal
    sausage (torciniello) 263
    Sautéed lamb offal 60
Lasagne Marche style 10, 62
Lauro Rossi Theatre, Macerata 35
Le virtù 150
lemon
    Almond and lemon biscotti 70
    Crostini with lemon ricotta
        and spinach 210
    Crustacea with lemon, garlic
        and parsley sauce 248
    Egg, lemon and cheese
        sauce 163
    Gratinated prawns with
        lemon and parsley 40
    Lamb with egg, lemon
        and cheese sauce 163
    Lemon and ricotta
        ring cake 69, 77, 181

lentils
    Broken pasta and lentil soup 143
    Cereal soup 150
    Lentil and capsicum salad 237
    puy 237
lettuce
    Stewed peas with prosciutto
        and baby lettuce 30
Levi, Primo 77

M

*Maccheroni alla chitarra con fiori
    di zucca e zafferano* 117
Macerata 51
    truffles 10
Marche region 2, 9–73
    agriturismi 60
    cheeses 34
    cuisine 10, 22, 54, 62
    farro (spelt) 12
    history 16
    Mistrà liqueur 66
    Montecassiano 15–17
    name 65
    recipes 18–66
    seafood 10, 36
    truffles 10, 34
    wine 10
Marina di San Vito 122–5
Mascarpone cream 188
meat *see* beef; lamb; pork; sausages;
    sheep; veal
Minestrone primavera 33
Mini sheep skewers 159
Mistrà liqueur 66
Molise 5, 195–275
    antipasti 263
    cuisine 196, 202, 238
    dairy industry 34
    dialect 240
    goat meat 252
    onion festival 243
    pasta 252
    Pietrabbondante 196–7, 272–4
    products 196, 202
    recipes 205–70
    seafood 248
    stone-wall villages 196
    transhumance 261
    truffles 34
    wines 202
Monkfish ragù 10, 42
Montecassiano 15–17
Montesilvano 110
Mostaccioli 264
mozzarella 263
'mpepata di cozze 138
mushrooms
    Cereal soup 150
    Woodsman's chicken 59
mussels
    Homemade spaghetti with
        stuffed mussels 128
    Mussels in pepper broth 138
    vacuum-packed 138

N

No-knead spelt pizza
    with soppressata
    and potatoes 212
Nonna Irene 148, 170
Nonno Domenico 148, 188
noodles
    Handmade noodles
        with monkfish
        ragù 10, 42
    Noodles with zucchini
        blossom and saffron
        sauce 117
nutmeg 210
nuts
    Flourless walnut cake 268
    see also almonds

O

octopus
    cleaning 246
    Octopus and potato
        salad 10, 46
    Octopus in purgatory
        (aka spicy baby
        octopus stew) 246
    shopping for 46
offal
    sausage (torciniello) 263
    Sautéed lamb offal 60
oil
    Chilli oil 127
    see also olive oil
Olive all'ascolana 10, 22
olive oil
    Apricot and olive oil
        cake 66
    Olive oil bread crescents 206
    olive oil pastry 108
    replacing butter 66
    Savoury white wine and
        olive oil waffles 90
olives
    Stuffed fried olives 10, 22
onions
    Focaccia with stewed
        onion 18
    onion festival, Molise 243
    Onion stew 243
    Sweet and sour capsicum 112

P

Pallotte cacio e ovo 92
Pan dell'orso 178
pancetta in soups 33
Panini all'olio 206
parrozzo 178
parsley
    Gratinated prawns
        with lemon and
        parsley 40
    Lemon, garlic and
        parsley sauce 248

pasta
    Antonina's cannelloni with
        braised meat 157
    Broken pasta and lentil
        soup 143
    cavatelli lunghi 254
    Ditalini with clams and chickpeas,
        cooked risotto-style 140
    factories 77–8
    Fresh pasta strips with slow-
        cooked goat sauce 252
    Handmade pasta with
        slow-cooked
        meat sauce 254
    Homemade pasta squares
        with fish stew 126
    Homemade spaghetti with
        stuffed mussels 128
    Homemade tagliolini with
        sea urchin roe 244
    Lasagne Marche style 10, 62
    malefante 252
    Pasta and bean soup 148
    Pasta dough 149
    see also noodles
Pasta rotta con lenticchie 143
pastries
    Chickpea and honey
        pastries 170
    Filled short pastries 176
    Grape jam crescents 166
    see also tarts
pastry
    Almond short pastry 224
    olive oil pastry 108
Patate arrosto con alloro
    e guanciale 52
peaches
    Wine-drenched peaches with
        mascarpone cream 188
peas
    Lamb in broth with peas and
        broad beans 258
    Stewed peas with prosciutto
        and baby lettuce 30
Pentro 202
Peperonata 112
Peperoni imbottiti 230
Pescara 178
Pesche di Castelbottaccio 266
Pesche al vino con crema di
    mascarpone 188
Pescocostanzo 234
Pietrabbondante 196–7, 272–4
Piselli, prosciutto e lattuga 30
pizza
    dough 132
    No-knead spelt pizza
        with soppressata
        and potatoes 212
    Seafood pizza 132
    tips 132
Pizza dolce 182
Pizza di farro con soppressata
    e patate 212
Pizza con frutti di mare 132

Pizza rustica con bietola 108
Pizza di San Martino 205
Pizza scima 86
Pizzelle salate con vino 90
polenta
    Soft polenta 59
Polipo con patate 46
Pollo alla boscaiola 59
Pollo in potacchio 56
pork
    Handmade pasta with slow-cooked
        meat sauce 254
    Lasagne Marche style 10, 62
    Roast potatoes with bay leaves
        and cured pork cheek 52
    Slow-cooked meat sauce 254
    Stuffed fried olives 10, 22
potatoes
    No-knead spelt pizza with
        soppressata and potatoes 212
    Octopus and potato salad 10, 46
    Potato chips 60
    Potato gnocchi with zucchini
        and pecorino 28
    Roast potatoes with bay leaves
        and cured pork cheek 52
    Woodsman's chicken 59
potato starch 182, 183
prawns
    Crispy fried prawns and calamari 39
    Gratinated prawns with
        lemon and parsley 40
    using heads and tails 133
Primo sale 218
Primo sale alla piastra con verdure 220
primo sale cheese
    Grilled primo sale and
        vegetable salad 220
    Homemade primo sale
        cheese 202, 216, 218
prosciutto
    Stewed peas with prosciutto
        and baby lettuce 30

R

rabbit
    deboning 54
    Rolled deboned rabbit 10, 54
ragù
    Fresh pasta strips with slow-
        cooked goat sauce 252
    Monkfish ragù 10, 42
raviggiolo cheese 34
Raw artichoke and shaved pecorino
    salad 99
Recanati 59, 62
ricotta
    buying 230
    Crostini with lemon ricotta
        and spinach 210
    Homemade ricotta 216, 218, 223
    Lemon and ricotta ring
        cake 69, 77, 181
    Ricotta, chocolate and cherry tart 224
    Vincenzo's fiadone cake 181

Ricotta fatta in casa 223
Roast potatoes with bay leaves
    and cured pork cheek 52
Roccascalegna 80, 86
Rolled deboned rabbit 10, 54

S

saffron
    Saffron custard 174
    Saffron sauce 117
    Saffron tartlets 174
Sagne e fasciul' 77, 148
Saint Martin rolls 205
salads
    Grilled primo sale and
        vegetable salad 220
    Lentil and capsicum salad 237
    Octopus and potato salad 10, 46
    Raw artichoke and shaved
        pecorino salad 99
salami
    No-knead spelt pizza
        with soppressata and
        potatoes 212
sambuca 66, 181
San Benedetto del Tronto 36, 48
sauces
    Béchamel sauce 63
    Egg, lemon and cheese
        sauce 163
    Lemon, garlic and
        parsley sauce 248
    Saffron sauce 117
    Slow-cooked goat sauce 252
    Slow-cooked meat sauce 254
    Tomato sauce 128, 157
sausages 77
    ciauscolo 34
    Slow-cooked meat sauce 254
    torciniello 263
Sautéed artichokes 102
Sautéed lamb offal 60
Savoury tart with chard 108
Savoury white wine and olive oil
    waffles 90
scamorza 157, 227
Science in the Kitchen and the Art of
    Eating Well 268
Scrippelle 'mbusse 144
seafood
    Crustacea with lemon,
        garlic and parsley
        sauce 248
    Fritto misto 10, 39
    Homemade tagliolini with
        sea urchin roe 244
    San Benedetto del Tronto 36
    Seafood pizza 132
    see also calamari; clams; mussels;
        octopus; prawns
Sergio, Signor 125
sheep's meat
    Mini sheep skewers 159
    Sheep stew 261
Signora Pia's apple cake 270

skewers
  Mini sheep skewers 159
Slow-cooked goat sauce 252
Slow-cooked meat sauce 254
Soft polenta 59
soppressata
  No-knead spelt pizza with
    soppressata and potatoes 212
soups
  adding pancetta or speck 33
  Broken pasta and lentil
    soup 143
  Cereal soup 150
  farro in 12
  Mussels in pepper broth 138
  Pasta and bean soup 148
  Spring vegetable minestrone 33
  see also broth
spelt flour 212
  Spelt ciabatta 12, 20
Spicy baby octopus stew 246
spinach
  Crostini with lemon ricotta
    and spinach 210
sponge cakes
  Celebration sponge cake 182
  Sponge cakes from
    Castelbottaccio 266
Spring vegetable minestrone 33
squid *see* calamari
Stale bread and pecorino
  dumplings 92
stews
  Chickpea stew 238
  Homemade pasta squares
    with fish stew 126
  Lamb in broth with peas
    and broad beans 258
  Octopus in purgatory (aka spicy
    baby octopus stew) 246
  Onion stew 243
  Sheep stew 261
  Stewed peas with prosciutto
    and baby lettuce 30
Strozzapreti con rana pescatrice 42
struffoli *see* Cicerchiata 184
Stuffed capsicum 230
Stuffed fried olives 10, 22
Sweet and sour capsicum 112

T

Tacconcelli con ragù di pesce 126
Tagliolini ai ricci di mare 244
Tartellette allo zafferano 174
tarts, savoury
  Savoury tart with chard 108
tarts, sweet
  Ricotta, chocolate and
    cherry tart 224
  Saffron tartlets 174
Termoli 200, 244
toasted ground almonds 167
tomatoes
  Braised chicken marylands
    with wine and tomatoes 56

Calamari with tomatoes and wine 45
Cereal soup 150
Handmade pasta with slow-cooked
  meat sauce 254
Lasagne Marche style 10, 62
Stale bread and pecorino
  dumplings 92
Sweet and sour capsicum 112
Tomato sauce 128, 157
torciniello 263
Torricella Peligna 2, 7, 77, 86, 92, 145,
  155, 166, 170, 181
Torta all'olio e albicocche 66
Torta di mele della signora Pia 270
Torta di noci e cioccolato 268
Tortino di carciofi gratinato 96, 100
Tozzetti 70
trabocchi 137
transhumance 89, 261
Troilo, Antonina 152, 153
truffles 10, 34

V

veal
  Antonina's cannelloni with
    braised meat 157
vegetables
  farmers' markets 24, 96
  Grilled primo sale and
    vegetable salad 220
  Spring vegetable minestrone 33
  see also specific vegetables
vegetarian
  Artichoke gratin 96, 100
  Spring vegetable minestrone 33
  Stewed peas with prosciutto and
    baby lettuce 30
Venafro 263
Villetta Barrea 74
vin cotto 243
vin santo 62
Vincenzo's fiadone cake 181
Vincisgrassi 10, 62

W

waffles
  Savoury white wine and
    olive oil waffles 90
whey 216, 223
White wine unleavened bread 86
wine 10
  Abruzzo region 77
  Braised chicken marylands with
    wine and tomatoes 56
  Calamari with tomatoes and wine 45
  digestives 77
  Mussels in pepper broth 138
  Savoury white wine and olive oil
    waffles 90
  vin santo 62
  White wine unleavened bread 86
  Wine-drenched peaches with
    mascarpone cream 188
Woodsman's chicken 59

Y

yoghurt
  Homemade primo sale
    cheese 202, 216, 218

Z

zucchini 39
  Potato gnocchi with zucchini
    and pecorino 28
  Zucchini gratin 27
zucchini flowers
  Noodles with zucchini blossom
    and saffron sauce 117
Zucchine gratinate 27
Zuppa di cipolle 243

LANTERN

Published by the Penguin Group
Penguin Group (Australia)
707 Collins Street, Melbourne, Victoria 3008, Australia
(a division of Penguin Australia Pty Ltd)
Penguin Group (USA) Inc.
375 Hudson Street, New York, New York 10014, USA
Penguin Group (Canada)
90 Eglinton Avenue East, Suite 700, Toronto,
Canada ON M4P 2Y3
(a division of Penguin Canada Books Inc.)
Penguin Books Ltd
80 Strand, London WC2R 0RL England
Penguin Ireland
25 St Stephen's Green, Dublin 2, Ireland
(a division of Penguin Books Ltd)
Penguin Books India Pvt Ltd
11 Community Centre, Panchsheel Park, New Delhi –
110 017, India
Penguin Group (NZ)
67 Apollo Drive, Rosedale, Auckland 0632, New Zealand
(a division of Penguin New Zealand Pty Ltd)
Penguin Books (South Africa) (Pty) Ltd, Rosebank Office
Park, Block D, 181 Jan Smuts Avenue, Parktown North,
Johannesburg, 2196, South Africa
Penguin (Beijing) Ltd
7F, Tower B, Jiaming Center, 27 East Third Ring Road North,
Chaoyang District, Beijing 100020, China

Penguin Books Ltd, Registered Offices: 80 Strand, London,
WC2R 0RL, England

First published by Penguin Group (Australia), 2014

10 9 8 7 6 5 4 3 2 1

Text copyright © Silvia Colloca 2014
Recipe photography copyright © Chris Chen 2014
Location photography copyright © Carla Coulson 2014

Internal design by Evi O. © Penguin Group (Australia)
Illustrations by Jesse Chick
Handwriting by Charlotte Bachali
Recipe photography by Chris Chen
Location photography by Carla Coulson
Styling by Cass Stokes and Jane Hann
Typeset in Dante by Post Pre-Press Group,
Brisbane, Queensland
Colour separation by
Splitting Image Colour Studio, Clayton, Victoria
Printed and bound in China by
1010 Printing International Limited

Made In Italy with Silvia Colloca™ is a trademark of, and is
licensed by FremantleMedia Australia. All rights reserved.

National Library of Australia
Cataloguing-in-Publication data:

Colloca, Silvia, author.
Made in Italy / Silvia Colloca;
photography by Chris Chen and Carla Coulson.
ISBN: 9781921383977 (hardback)
Cooking, Italian.
Italy – Description and travel.
Chen, Chris, photographer.
Coulson, Carla, photographer.

641.5945

penguin.com.au/lantern

Sunrise over Val di Sangro